To Libby

Helping Yourself Grow Old

Things I Said to Myself
When I was Almost Ninety

Frances Fuller

Treehouse Publishing

Helping Yourself Grow Old

Things I Said to Myself
When I was Almost Ninety

Frances Fuller

Published by Treehouse Publishing
Placerville CA

© Copyright - Frances Fuller. All rights reserved.
First Paperback Printing November 2019

Publisher: Treehouse Publishing

ISBN: 978-0-9987996-3-6

Cover Design: Treehouse Publishing

Back Cover Design: Treehouse Publishing

Originally published in the USA by Treehouse Publishing
Placerville CA

Treehouse Publishing

Table Of Contents

I Will Just Do It

I Will Give Myself a Break

I Will Forgive

I Will Tell Stories

What My Scars Say

I Will Be Responsible for Health

I Will Keep Growing

I Will Relinquish Control

Leaving Home

I Will Take the Initiative

I Will Have a Bad Day

I Will Face the Truth

I Will Choose Again

Traveling by Remembering

I Will Celebrate

I Will Bless My Grandchildren

I Will Say Goodbye

I Will Trust God with the End

Today I Am Ninety

Dedication

This work is dedicated to Tim, Jan, Jim, Dwight and Cynthia, five good reasons for the thoughts in this book

Acknowledgements

Some influences are hard to measure, though without them nothing would be done.

My local library, a branch of the El Dorado County Public Library, urges me on, by connecting me with other writers, by staging public events and inviting me to speak, teach, sell, and by always asking: What are you working on?

My little writing group, three other women, read portions of this book. Jo, Joy, and Sallie were encouragers, telling me frankly what was good and what could be better. And at the end Sallie read the completed manuscript with the eye of an editor. (All silly mistakes will turn out to be places where I failed to take her advice.)

The Northern California Publishers and Authors organization and its members always support me with information and affirmation.

Joyce, one of the smartest people I know, committed to forming a discussion group of elderly people who will read the book together, far away in Holland, Michigan. Elderly people waiting in cities I have never seen is a reason to keep working.

Don, who knows almost everything I don't know about making a book, spent hours on the phone answering my questions.

My own children claim that this work is urgent.

Except for all of these people, the publication of my thoughts when I was almost ninety is my own fault.

Preface

For several months of my eighty-eighth year I concentrated my reading on books about aging. In the process I noticed that there seemed to be none written by really old people. A seventy year old did a beautiful job but admitted that she was only in the first of three stages of growing old. And I found several excellent books by people qualified academically to write about places in life they had never actually been.

Subconsciously, I maybe was looking for memoirs, because I really like memoirs. Then I noticed in Mary Karr's book, *The Art of Memoir*, a statement to the effect that no one should write about an experience until it is at least seven years past, because one does not have genuine perspective on the past for at least that long.

No wonder, I thought, that there are no memoirs about eighty-five and on, the final stage of aging. One cannot tell herself on her ninetieth birthday, I must wait seven more years before I write about this.

And since I was the one who wanted a book I just mentally addressed it to myself and plunged in. I suppose that makes this more diary than memoir. It is a story written out of the middle whose end the author does not know. I chose a quitting place, and already there have been surprises.

My life is a bit like this autumn in California, an autumn that refuses to give up summer. The ground is ankle-deep in leaves, yet every time I look up from this keyboard, I see small, slow showers of yellow leaves.

Introduction: Figuring It Out

When I started writing this series of essays all I wanted was just not to be a nuisance. I had not lived alone for sixty-three years and suddenly was a widow. Problems kept jumping on me. The property insurance company said I had to conform to fire department guidelines by cutting down all my shade trees. The washing machine wobbled. The house popped and creaked at night. I didn't know where to buy pellets for my new stove, or how much to pay. Nobody hugged me in the morning.

I was eighty-eight and for the first time it occurred to me that I was old. This meant, I assumed, that I was on a downhill slope. Nothing was going to get easier. What I wanted was simple, just to handle life without nagging somebody every day.

A friend wrote me a sympathetic note. She said, "We can buy a how-to book on everything in the world except how to get old and die gracefully." Something close to that, she said.

I grabbed on to the challenge. I would figure it out and write it. I would try doing what I wrote. And keep writing it down. When I had discovered how to get old and die without complicating other people's lives, I would give the secret to the world. A how-to book.

Except I never much liked how-to books. And I really hate being didactic.

Maybe I could just tell the truth: that this is what I thought when I was eighty-eight.

Old . . . this is what most people are going to be eventually.

So I began. I sat down to this laptop sure of what I meant to do and wrote this sentence: Now that I am eighty-eight there are just two big things I need to know: how to stay in the world without being a nuisance and how to leave the world gracefully.

With this "thesis sentence" in place I began to seek the elements of the two things I needed to know. I was on a search now, seeking practical wisdom about how to live.

While I worried about fire insurance and watched all my shade trees being cut down, I found a washing-machine repairman, googled where to buy pellet fuel, learned to do without hugs and started a rambling diary about being old.

Several things happened, beside the fact that I wrote a lot of nonsense. I started to feel great empathy for other people who feel a little bit lost in their lives. And I caught on that my proposed thesis might be a bit humorous and catchy, but it fell obviously short of saying what I truly need to know.

It is true that I don't want to be a nuisance. Most of us old people are afraid of that, I suspect. I did develop an outline based on that introductory sentence. Each chapter was a promise to my family and to myself; each promise was, I hoped, at least a partial solution to a problem. But slowly I understood that its points were mostly applicable to an upside down view of life.

For instance, since one of the promises I was making was to throw away my own trash before I leave, I started spending time sorting all the paper in my files, separating trash from items somebody besides me might need (plus things I am hopelessly attached to). This required reading a lot of old correspondence. That's how I came across a quote from me to my children. The year was 1983. I had been in the U.S. for a year and was back in Lebanon, trying to lead a publishing house functioning in the middle of a civil war. And I wrote, "Everyone here is spending most of his time trying to solve a mountain of problems. I have decided to ignore problems and focus on ways to get my job done anyway. It is amazing how much difference this approach makes."

This bit of sense from my own younger self helped me to wake up and see the light.

I may be old, but I have my gifts, my years of experience, my deep concerns, a life story full of sense and nonsense (some of which I have discovered) and desires that get me out of bed in the morning. I do not get up looking for a way to avoid bothering somebody. I get up with an agenda, an intention, a chosen responsibility and resources to work with.

Old age is, I admit, full of problems. As in civil war, we spend a lot of time on emergencies, but the emergencies are not the point. There is a reason we are here in the middle of this struggle.

This called for a manuscript revision. Now I say that the two things I need to know are: how to live with purpose and how to die in peace.

Even in my original outline, one of my promises was to live with purpose. But then I was thinking of purpose as merely a way not to be a nuisance. That it may be, but purpose has a much bigger role than that. Purpose will grow out of who I am. Well chosen, purpose will align me with my gifts and with my spirituality. Purpose will make me a constructive member of society. Purpose will motivate me, may even give me peace with myself. Purpose will take control of my to-do list, promoting value in place of busyness. Purpose will empower me to overcome obstacles and weaknesses.

While each promise in my original outline was supposed to be an action that prevented my being a nuisance, now I must examine each on the basis of very personal intentions propelling the rest of my life. For instance, from the beginning I claimed I would keep house. And I said I would accept my limitations and ask for help. I thought that doing these things would prevent my being a worry to my children. These two ideas will stay in my outline, because I see how they deepen my own life. They will stay also because of the ways they affect my relationship with others, enabling me to go on contributing to the life of my family and community. I like the idea of service and example so much better than just not being a nuisance.

I record now these details from the process I am in, because writing is the way I am finding a path through this unfamiliar terrain. I do want to discover for myself how to live long without being a burden to those I love and how to leave in a way that gives them peace. I see that old age, like youth and the prime of life, like even the place we live—Planet Earth herself, is a jumble of valleys and mountains, sunny meadows and spooky forests, stunning views and lonely deserts. I have in my long life faced disasters, and I have enjoyed some grand moments. Most of what I know I learned by getting in and out of trouble. Tomorrow I may fall into a crevasse or shelter in a cozy cave. In either I may find a clue to the next step.

Or maybe I will just need a new pair of boots. And courage to throw this page away and start over. While I think it through, I will write.

Getting to Know My Aging Self

So long as there were two of us I did not know that I was old.

Two people together can combine their abilities. As always, Wayne could do things I couldn't do; I could do things he couldn't do. That left fewer things that no one could do and fewer reasons to acknowledge the truth.

When he was confused I noticed. This didn't need a lot of smarts. Having been missing for a couple of hours, he came in the house covered with sawdust, not in itself too unusual for a Fuller, a member of a tribe who consider themselves pioneers, always hacking away at the forest. But to come in the house covered with sawdust and say, "I dreamed I was cutting wood," this should not sound quite normal to any wife.

Hoping to clarify his mind and solve a mystery, I took him up the road to an empty lot where he and a friend had felled trees a week before. In front of us was the evidence of work done since then, and the scent of fresh pine sap sweetened the air. He stood there with sawdust in his white hair, on the shoulders of his blue shirt, on the tops of his shoes, and insisted that he was not the one who had stripped the limbs and cut that

1

tree into rounds. It was true that the chainsaw was in the trunk of his car, but he had not used it.

I took him to the ER. All the way he asked me where we were going and why.

The trip resulted in his getting the defibrillator that saved his life multiple times in the next ten years. All those years were time we borrowed, beyond life expectancy, 78.7 years in 2018.

But that afternoon of confusion resulted from a fragile heart, not old age. On the other hand, old age and fragile hearts get together, developing a chicken-and-egg relationship, creating this syndrome of weaknesses.

It is all very confusing and creepy and subtle. How could I be expected to know that we were old? Maybe he was old, but me too?

It did not arrive like a birthday, true one day but not the day before. Nor did it reach us claiming a precise definition. It insinuated itself into our healthy bodies and robust minds, imitating a strained back, a bad dream, a depleted hormone, a mental slip, a midday lethargy.

Discipline and determination filled in some gaps. The same man who shuffled through the house in bedroom slippers kept our property clean, raking and blowing, trimming, weeding, piling, burning, by doing a little every day, by working an hour and taking a break. He fixed leaky faucets, oiled squeaky doors, paid the taxes, got up early to make the coffee, remembered anniversaries and, in order, with relevant dates, all the kings and prophets of Israel and the significance of their stories. In between, he wrote the story of his family.

He did remark apologetically about the loss of muscles in his arms and legs. I think he missed his young beautiful body. He did say a few times something a little trite and sad about old age not being fun. I think I tended to ignore such remarks. Maybe that was wrong.

He also quit driving the car, and he loved to drive. He was a better driver than I, and we both knew it. Suspicious maybe of passing symptoms, a lightness in his head, a kick from the defibrillator (I don't know, he didn't say) just one day as we went out to the car, he said, "Would you like to drive?" And that was it. He sat beside me and watched the scenery go by, for the next couple of years.

He was not gone a month before I noticed all the things I couldn't do. It wasn't, I realized, just a matter of lifestyle that he did some jobs and I did others. Mostly, the division of labor was about what we could do or what we were good at doing.

First I didn't know what to do when the washing machine wobbled. Then I knew that knowing didn't help. I couldn't stop that wobble, and it was now very late to learn to repair washing machines. I couldn't even put a new lightbulb into the recessed receptacle above my rocking chair. Or could I? The truth is that I have osteoporosis and cannot afford to fall, which means no standing on stools, no climbing into chairs, no lifting boxes full of old paper, no speeding on the stairs.

Cautious becomes a way of living. Not because I am old; because I have osteoporosis. But what's the difference? I had good bones once when I was young.

Old age and bad health are not identical twins, just best friends who live together in symbiotic harmony.

This is not a medical diagnosis, nor is it a sociological study. I am not capable of either. It is my effort to be forthright about lasting beyond the normal expiration date, an adventure I had no right to expect and did not anticipate.

I Will Live with Purpose

A certain man came to our grief support group only once. He came in a wheelchair. Somebody removed an ordinary straight chair from the circle so that he could maneuver into its spot.

Only once he spoke.

"I am lost," he said. "I get up in the morning, put on my clothes and sit in my chair. I can't think of anything else to do. I don't know why I am here."

Immediately when he said it I saw that what he had lost was absolutely vital to his survival.

There was a back story, of course. His wife had dementia. For several years he was her caretaker, responsible for her health and happiness. He prepared her food, kept her clean, brushed her hair, measured her medicine, drove her to the doctor. Now she was gone. His life work was done.

Losses can do that to any of us. Like turning onto a road that ends at a locked barricade, death feels at first like a mistake. Months after the fact I keep wondering how I could have known my husband's illness was terminal and then not expected that moment. I had made a careful plan for a day that never came.

There are other things that might bring us to such a barricade. Retirement did it to my daddy. A carpenter for the Missouri Pacific Railroad, he was so tired of lifting and drilling and nailing and shouting into the wind. So tired of the sun on his skin, the cold in his bones and cinders blowing in his face. So weary of living on a boxcar and cooking while starving. So tired of leaving home every Sunday afternoon and riding trains to places with names that made his children laugh. Retired at last, he fell into his easy chair, picked up the newspaper and disappeared behind it.

"You're fired" is something that will work to bring you to the barricade. Getting dumped by your sweetheart. Losing your religion. Even a happy thing: a new understanding of life, marriage, a job offer, news that a baby is on the way, a goal reached will require changing course, finding another road, looking again at the map, one's focus. A finer intention.

The "barricade" may be like the fire escape gate on my road. The padlock on the chain means nothing. I can lift the chain over the post, pull away the gate and drive across my neighbor's field to the highway in seconds. With flames at my back, the "barricade" becomes a way out of here.

Nothing has brought me face to face with my purposes like discovering that I am almost ninety. I don't think I have an ancestor who has lived past ninety. I was with my mother on her ninetieth birthday, and that was the last time I saw her alive.

If I last longer than others it won't be the first time I broke a family rule, but I am not in control. Every day is a gift now. What do I want to do with it?

To clarify my purpose is imperative, because there

are, I discover, things I still want for myself and others. All of it seems to come together under two big umbrellas:

I want to be finally the person I am supposed to be.

And I want to make life easier or at least richer for those I love.

These motives are behind the undertaking of this book in ways that will, I hope, become obvious.

On my tack board I have a quote attributed to a homeless man in Los Angeles: "When you have nothing planned, that's when depression sets in." I took that from a newspaper article, astonished momentarily to think that even a homeless man camping out on the street might have a plan, a way forward, something to think about and apply himself to.

I have always had a to-do list. Making it, on the night before when I am efficient, sometimes a week ahead to fit it with my calendar, is routine. It is detailed. Appointments go on first. Bible study at my church has been on Wednesday morning for years, but I still write it down. The list tells me to put out the trash. Otherwise, I might forget. The day's menu is on there. Without it I tend to just get hungry and eat a bag of nuts. I let the spinach die. Routine things are on there, because they take time.

One of my problems is that certain things on my list will try to take over. If I give writing two hours, it will take three and then it is too late to call the friend I have been neglecting.

But I have to be careful not to get mixed up here. A to-do list is not a plan, a plan is not a goal, a goal is not a purpose. These must come in the opposite order.

A purpose is a cause needing a goal; the goal has to be measurable so we will know when we have achieved it; a plan is a path to the goal; a work list names steps in the plan. I know a little bit about how to sort this out when I am talking about running a club or creating a product. When the project is my life, it gets harder; it changes shape like a foam pillow when I punch it or rest my head on it; it fades under different kinds of light.

Sometimes my list has nothing to do with what I have claimed as a life purpose. Some items may be only what I feel obligated to do whether I want to or not.

Years ago when I lived in Lebanon in the middle of a civil war, frustrated almost daily by obstacles to getting my work done, I was often annoyed by letters from America. People invariably shared lists of activities and then the summary: "We keep busy." The frequency with which this little sentence appeared in end-of-the-year newsletters was alarming. The obvious goal of life in America was to keep busy.

This turns out to be a communicable disease.

We do. I do. Keep busy.

Keeping busy makes me feel I am going somewhere.

Months ago I wrote down these words: "Everybody is allowed one big, squishy immeasurable goal. That's a purpose." I don't remember where I got that; I don't think I made it up.

The reason I like it is that it seems true in a slippery sort of way. I find that I am serious about the way I want to live, now that I am almost ninety, but my two purposes keep falling apart into numerous pieces that beg for definition.

I intend to live with purpose and to share some of them on these pages in the form of bold claims about what I will do. I know that writing them down and sharing them turns them into promises, and somewhere I'm bound to fail. That's why I like that word "squishy." It gives me room to try to be more than I am and to figure it out as I go.

This is probably the most important thing I have to say and the single most vital element in aging well. I hope so, because it is my clearest thought.

I expect to live with purpose.

I Will Live with Gratitude

This kind of thing happens to women in beauty shops. With an unfamiliar sort of apron, tied around our necks, wet hair and pale, wrinkled faces exposed by the lights and mirrors, we submit to being both vulnerable and pampered. The room is full of chatter and the comfortable companionship of women who either understand or don't care anyway. And we talk.

Once I happened to get a new beautician, a warm, open woman about half my age. I'm going to say her name was Marge, though that is not quite right. While she shampooed and clipped and reshaped my hair with her clever brush and blower, I talked to Marge. I told her about my husband's death, about nearly losing my fire insurance, about some of the little difficulties of being alone and old.

Marge told me that she had reduced her work hours and put them all into two days of the week so she could be at home more, not for her husband or her teenager but for her mother-in-law who lived beside them in an RV. In a few carefully chosen words, she acknowledged that the elderly woman was a problem and a handful.

This sounded like something I needed to hear, so I confessed that I was getting older fast and dreaded becoming a problem to my family.

I asked her, "What can I do to keep from being a nuisance? Give me some tips."

Then, lifting a lock of my hair and clipping just the thin ends, Marge explained that her mother-in-law was never quite happy with services she received. She always wanted more than her son and his wife could give, and she never said, "Thank you."

Because she was so demanding, they actually wrote a contract, something I would never have imagined. The document named what they would do for her and what they would provide, for instance, how many cigarettes they would buy her every month. Marge and her husband signed the contract, promising what they would do for her, and she signed, promising to be satisfied with that.

Then, would you believe it? The old lady went to the store with her daughter-in-law and managed to get to the checkout stand with two cartons of cigarettes instead of the one she was due.

I am not worried about something like that, but I have noticed that it would be easy to become a complainer.

The early morning is the hardest for me, because I wake daily to the news that I am alone. Basically not a morning person anyway, I wobble out to the living room where for so many years my husband met me with a hug and told me, "Sit here. The coffee water is hot."

I would sit in my favorite chair and he would bring my cup of caffeine, steaming the way I like it. See, I am spoiled.

But the problem is not coffee delivered to my chair. I am not helpless. I can just pass through this room, and in five minutes be back, sitting in the rocker with the cup in my hand. Then the emptiness in the room will invade my chest where it weighs a ton.

To rescue myself I name the things for which I am thankful.

I usually start with the simplest things, little, eminent, visible things. My cup of coffee. The weather. The pictures on the wall, each with some special meaning in my life. The flowers from a friend. The books I am reading. I don't assume anything is automatic and will always be mine.

I think of my family, the things they do for me. I name my grandchildren, one by one, marvel at their personalities and skills and entreat God to bless them.

I remember experiences: a conversation I had with someone, an idea that came to me, an event I am looking forward to. My friends. What would I do without my friends?

Right now while writing this, I become grateful, for basic things.

Home. I am not a refugee. I have a country, a house, my own room and a comfortable bed to sleep in.

The leftovers in the fridge. No need to cook today and no famine here.

My gratitude for these basic things is enhanced by recent events. Not far from here nearly six thousand homes were destroyed these last ten days in the inferno that swept through the wine country at incredible speed. The fire started in the middle of the night when people were asleep. Some elderly people were unable to move fast enough to escape. I am not more deserving or more loved than any of those people. I am just fortunate. This time.

While they suffered, this forested area I live in was under a red flag warning. A spark could have reduced everything I have to ashes. I am not proud or gloating. I am just saying that I was blessed.

Sometimes gratitude is a natural acknowledgement of what we could have lost and didn't.

It occurs to me that having lived a long time and survived so much gives us old people a special ability to be thankful. Our years have been full of things that could have happened and did not. We were sick unto death and got well. We were one minute behind the six-car pileup in which cars burned and people died. We were in a disastrous relationship but got ourselves out. We were penniless in a strange city and somebody gave us a job. Disaster struck, but we were surrounded by caring friends.

Just by remembering, we can say thanks all day long.

Not only that, but the world we live in recognizes in various ways the handicaps of age and gives us a break here and there. For instance, this year I hired a local company to clean up my property and make it as fireproof as possible. They sent three men to pick up all the little limbs that fell during the winter storms, put them through a chipper, blow all the fallen leaves into great mounds and burn them. They were skilled and thorough. They came on time and stayed until they could safely leave the fires they had set. Now I could drop a burning match anywhere on my lot, and the blaze would not travel from that spot, because the ground is clean, the grass is mown, low limbs on the trees have been stripped away.

And the bill I received gave me the benefit of a twenty percent senior discount.

We have grown accustomed to such favors. And they are favors. The men who came here to work in my yard are the same men who cleaned a lot of people's yards. They worked everywhere with the same diligence and efficiency. The company employs them at a certain salary that does not change from yard to yard, depending on the financial capabilities of the customer.

If someone sent me a check for two hundred dollars in a birthday card, I would write a thank you note. So I wrote a friendly note to the owner of that company and thanked him for the discount. It was part of my promise to live with gratitude.

Our gifts come from somewhere. The Christian scripture says, "Every good gift and every perfect gift comes down from the father . . ."

For the moment I forget the rest, but this is enough. The idea is that there is an ultimate Giver, responsible for all the good stuff, a generous Father, and this is so helpful, because I can't send a thank you note to an anonymous giver.

When I wake in the morning, the first words that move through my mind and then my lips are: "Thank you" for the night's rest, the new day, the things on my calendar, for feeling good.

When I get in bed at night the same. Thank you for the day, the work done, for the good tired feeling, the hot bath, such a great bed.

Midday is different. Sometimes I forget. I am hungry before lunch is ready, then I'm cranky and accuse myself of not caring about myself, I read the news and blame people and worry.

I remember when my children were like that. So cute in the mornings, so full of optimistic chatter over cereal and milk, and eagerness to start their day, so sweet in the evening after baths, so happy at story time, so sincere saying their childish prayers.

Midday was different in all the same ways.

Here in this old gold-mining town in the foothills of the Sierras we can't go anywhere without driving narrow, twisty, up and down roads. It can be a pain, but in our better moments we boast that every time we go anywhere we take the scenic route. On a trip I make frequently there is a connecting road, called Black Oak Mine Road, between two alternative ways to my destination. I love this little road, because about a third of it goes through a tunnel of trees. On either side the oaks and pines and madrone grow to the very edge of the road, so close together that their roots tangle in the soil and their branches mingle overhead, creating a canopy, one mile of shady seclusion. I can't even explain why I like this so much and look forward to it over and over.

It happened once, though, that I was driving with my thoughts somewhere else. I do that more than I would like to admit, but my car seems to know where I am going and rarely makes a mistake. That day I noticed that I had reached the park in the little town of Garden Valley, totally surprised to be there.

What happened to Black Oak Mine? I had started on 193 and now I was on Marshall Road. It was impossible to get from there to here without taking Black Oak Mine, but I had no memory of it.

I had missed the tunnel of trees! That made me mad at myself. It was as though I had been given a gift that I never opened.

This, I discover, is a common way to miss my blessings.

I am neither blind nor deaf; I just sometimes disconnect my senses from my consciousness and my heart.

Between every blessing and the pleasure it gives, there is the expectant response. I snip the ribbon and unwrap the gift and own it.

Without gratitude I have nothing.

That's why I am determined to walk through life alert, saying thank you.

And according to Marge, my favorite hairdresser, it will make me easier to live with.

In 1949 I was a student at Louisiana Tech. I lived with Grandmother Anderson who cooked my meals and made my clothes. While carrying a full academic load, I worked in a bakery thirty-five hours each week, earning a salary of fifty dollars at the end of each month. This was enough to recompense Grandmother for the expense of keeping me, plus a few dollars for other personal needs.

It happened once that I had a major need not covered by this fifty dollars. I needed ten dollars on a specific day. This was a lot of money in 1949. I had no idea where I could get it. Without it I was going to miss an experience that I wanted rather desperately. I was going to be embarrassed besides. Now I realize that borrowing the money did not occur to me. The culture in which I had grown up did not include borrowing or living on credit. We paid for what we needed as we obtained it; otherwise, we did not have it.

I really needed and wanted ten dollars, but I did not so much as talk about it. I did not tell my uncle who owned a grocery and must have had some liquid funds. I did not tell my grandmother. I was a Christian and knew how to take my problems to God, but I cannot claim that I prayed to find ten dollars. I do not remember it.

In the morning of the day that I needed the money by evening, I went to school penniless. At noon I came home for the lunch Grandmother had prepared for the two of us. There was mail in the box beside the front door, and I brought it in. One of the envelopes was for me, a letter from Mrs. Halk, a member of my hometown church. When I unfolded the one sheet of paper, a ten dollar bill fell out.

Mrs. Halk wrote me notes regularly. I think this was part of a project of the church women's group. They prayed for the church's young people who were away in school and sent little notes to encourage them. I received one from Mrs. Halk about once a month for two years. That day her note included, after her signature, a P.S. It said something like, "I'll bet you could use a few extra bucks." That was the only time she ever sent me money.

Obviously, I never forgot. The incident became to me a parable describing my life, illustrating the truth that everything I have has been a gift from someone, somewhere. Often I reflect on the Christian principle behind this, what it says about plenty and privilege. And poverty and power. The wealth of the universe, the generosity of nature, the character and expectations of God, the source of everything good and true.

Until now I am relieved and grateful, but after all these years, a feeling called gratitude seems meaningless, just a passing warmth.

"Thank you" can become a routine courtesy. Only words. The proof of its reality is generosity. As love requires appropriate actions, in a world full of needs gratitude requires giving. I cannot be both grateful and stingy.

My promise to live with gratitude must mean in the end that I will be generous.

I Will Be Who I Am

My mother told me . . .

I was three years old, playing in the small yard of our house on Levesque St. in the town where I was born. It was a Sunday morning.

A girl about sixteen years of age knocked on the door, and Mother answered. The girl said that she walked by our house every Sunday on her way to Sunday School down at the Baptist church. "Every Sunday," she told my mother, "this child is playing here, and I thought that I could easily take her with me."

This would be 1932. Trust in one another was a kind of assumption then, in small towns in the South like this one.

My mother told the girl that next week she would have me ready.

Of course I don't remember that first time. I was only three. But I remember that Sunday School. I remember women who squatted to hug me when I walked in the door. Always. One, in particular, had a large bosom. She pulled my face into this big, warm pillow and said happy words in my ear. There were other women who made little commotions of joy, happy to see me. They admired my dress; they touched my hair. I thought every week that my arrival made their day.

Keep in mind that I was only three and had two little sisters. There was no longer room for me in Mother's lap.

I learned that this was God's house and God loved me. I don't remember how this happened, except that we stood around the piano, the glorious piano, and sang. "Praise Him, Praise Him, all ye little children. God is love. God is love." And it was obvious. So obvious.

Now that I am old this is deep theology, so hard to explain. Then it was so simple. I was in God's house, and I was loved there, because that's the way God is.

Now I have a thousand questions. Every answer, every possible answer, raises another question. But don't misunderstand. My questions are rarely related to doubt. They are searchlights into our ignorance. They are expressions of awe and recognition of mystery, acknowledgements of things beyond knowing. They are questions about faith and how to live it out in the world. Often they are arguments with my fellow Christians.

When I started this book I thought it was a memoir. Sometimes it is, because I tell stories, some that happened long ago. But now I realize that this is more diary than memoir. Most days I write from the middle of the story, about growing old and winding down. My story is about learning daily to do this new thing.

For nearly ninety years I have been becoming what I am. This seems to require that you, the reader, know who is speaking. So I am trying to identify myself. This necessity has caused me to admit that, though I can still grow and intend to, I have been shaped by events and forces and circumstances beyond my control. I am the little girl taken to Sunday School by a stranger where I received love that I needed.

Still, I take responsibility for who I am, because of the conscious decisions I have made. I have had the opportunity to refuse what I was given, to change my mind, to go another direction. I chose, over and over, to accept that story of love instead of any alternative. I bet my life on it. I thrived on it.

And at some level beyond reasoning, I am convinced that nothing could ever undo what was done. I would be different without that knock on the door, if my mother had said, "You are kind, but . . .," if the women in that classroom had not cared and there had been no hugs, no story, no piano, no song.

This is the foundation story of who I am.

Reading this book will be easier now that you know.

Grieving

Four weeks ago today, in the evening, my husband died. He had been dying for months, disappearing at the alarming rate of a pound a day near the end, then leaving suddenly, in one second. His warm and loving, fragile heart simply stopped.

He said, "Wait just a minute," and fell backward. The moment seems to keep happening, leaving me waiting to know what he meant to do next. I have often wanted to turn the request around, because I keep thinking of little things I might do or say if I had one more minute. Honesty requires me to admit that I had sixty-three years and six months.

Everybody came, my loving family, who had just been here for a celebratory event. Barely home again, they turned their lives around to come back and weep together. We had the memorial service and buried his ashes in a little rural cemetery under a tree.

Together we planned what to write on the tombstone: "Well done, good and faithful servant."

A few days later, I made a long list of chores that had to be undertaken because of his departure. Since then I have been diligent, made a lot of phone calls, filled out forms, mailed notices and marked a dozen things done already.

Today, I attacked a boxful of assorted cards for birthdays, illnesses, anniversaries, just looking for envelopes I could use for my final batch of notices. And there it was, my undoing, a card I bought on some lost, forgotten day to give him the next June when people were honoring fathers. But I never gave it to him.

It is so perfect, expressing beautifully my love and admiration for the father of my children. I am talking about a love different from the love of children for their own father and somehow more basic, or more objective, than the love of a wife. It spoke of strength and softness. The message would have pleased him, made him happy.

There may have been in this century six men on the planet for whom this card is exactly right, and the one I loved never got it.

A friend who lost his mate several years ago had warned me about things like this. He advised me to throw out of my house little things that I might stumble over and then plunge into an emotional funk. I wondered how to find them in time but, honestly, I was not highly motivated to do that. I expected that they would be little objects that reminded me of happy memories and made me miss him more. I was not prepared to have my heart broken with regret.

Actually, Wayne didn't live until Father's Day this year, but that doesn't save me, since the card was purchased quite a while back, intended for some Father's Day now long past. Having recognized its appropriateness, I obviously bought it for the future, tucked it away and forgot it.

If he were here and I cried about such a failure, he would try to tell me it was nothing. In fact, we never thought it necessary to buy things, a card or a gift for every occasion. But I know he would have treasured that card and saved it in the book he made of our letters to one another. He kept everything: screws and boards, business letters, receipts, old X-rays of lungs and bones, as well as works of art by six-year-olds and a note I left on his pillow. Everything had value, either practical or sentimental. He was a rock, soft in the middle.

There must be a lesson in this story, one of those lessons we learn too late. But I can't state it or maybe I just can't bear to. I do suppose that in roundabout, bit by bit ways, I managed through the years to tell him the truths on this card, not just that he was loved but that he deserved it.

I thought for a while that I should throw the card away, so that it would never trip me up again, but I couldn't do it. I kept fighting an irrational, unstated hope that there was still a way to give it to him. I wondered, Should I go to the cemetery and leave it in a basket of flowers? That seemed a little ridiculous.

I decided finally to add it to his book of letters. Let history say at least that he was everything written in the card, and I knew it.

Grief, I have realized, is a natural and inevitable part of aging. It comes with the territory. If you get a lot of years, you get a lot of losses.

My husband was the youngest in his family, and he

had to give up all of them: his grandparents, parents, all his siblings and their mates.

I was born the first of four daughters. After our parents died the four of us made a habit of getting together some place for a week or so once a year. Now two of us are gone, and the youngest, widowed for a second time, fell and broke her leg. We talk on the phone occasionally, put news in an email.

Betty, Sterline, Julie and I became friends when we lived as students together in a small house in Berkeley. We did not choose but were assigned to one another by some impersonal system. Julie and I were roommates; Betty and Sterline shared the room next door. There were others in the building, but it was the four of us who somehow got glued together. Julie, who was Hungarian by way of Brazil and prone to charming errors of speech, dubbed us "The Four Muskets." On a trip to Lake Tahoe, somebody took a picture of the four of us, seated on a big rock with the lovely blue lake behind us, surrounded by snowy mountains. This picture became an icon, standing for the solidarity of friendship.

After only a year we began to scatter. Marriage, work, travel separated us, but we always found a way to come together again. Like my sisters and I, we had reunions, meeting in Virginia, Tennessee, California. And each time we staged another picture, in the same seating arrangement: Betty, Julie, I and then Sterline.

The last time was here in my home. Betty had COPD. Once I heard her coughing in an upstairs bedroom and I went up to see if I could help in any way. We sat on the edge of the bed in my yellow room. She leaned her head on my shoulder and said, "Frances, I am not getting better." The way I heard it was she knew she would never be better.

The next day we said goodbye. That was October. She died in February.

I agreed to speak at her memorial, but there was a snowstorm, and planes couldn't land anywhere near that little town. In the spring, Julie, Sterline and I went to Missouri to stand by her grave and to see from the road the little white house in which she grew up.

For several years Julie and I wondered what happened to Sterline. First she was forgetful and said strange things on the phone, then she disappeared out of our lives. Our letters didn't come back, but the phone number was out of service. Finally, we found her obituary.

Julie and I talk on the phone. She tells me that she has pictures of the four muskets in the drawer of her bedside table and opens it every morning to greet us. I have mine on the tack board behind my computer. She writes me small letters by hand.

Grief is part of the package. You get a lot of years, but some others get less, so we lose them.

I feel fortunate. Some of my friends have buried their children. The thought nearly makes my heart stop.

An unexpected part of this experience of grieving is my urge to clean up the world. It began when I purged my office of everything with the word cancer on it, all the brochures, all the information about help available, everything about chemo and reactions to it, doctors'

instructions, business cards, clinical trials, appointment schedules, support groups, hospice, even the phone numbers to call, if or when. I carried it all out of my house. In a hurry I took it, compelled to throw it into the recycling bin and drag it to the curb.

Of course, this is not the first time I ever had the urge to declutter. Such a mood is sometimes provoked by impatience with objects out of place or by the discovery that a few of my refrigerator dishes have become separated from their lids. This practical, get-organized mood is not what I am talking about. I am talking about a frantic need to put out of sight, beyond the possibility of finding again, everything that is breaking my heart. But I don't know where to stop.

In an effort to purge illness and death from my house, I attack all kinds of neglected clutter: objects not used, pens going dry, a blouse with a little rip, shoes that pinch my toes, old receipts and personal letters, even books I have finished with, some without reading.

After that, it is dirt. Between the windows and their screens, I see dirt, hateful dirt. When have I washed this narrow strip of metal? The groove the sliding door exposes when I push the door open is dirty. This seems obscene. And physically challenging for an old woman with a backache. There is a spider web in a corner beyond the reach of my fuzzy web catcher. A smear on a window pane. Pine pollen on the skylights. Wherever I sit I see something that steps on an exposed nerve, most of it beyond my ability to change.

In a meditative mood I ponder the connection between cancer and disorder and dirt. And a memory appears in my head, a long forgotten moment. Wayne and I were in a marriage enrichment conference. The leader had instructed each of us to make a list of the other's values, just writing them down in the order in which they came to mind. We had done this and now we were sitting side by side to look at these lists. Number One on the list of my values, as they had occurred to Wayne that morning was: beauty and cleanliness.

I remember looking at him with some amazement and gratitude.

When he was taking chemo, the medical people instructed me that the compromise of his immune system made necessary extreme measures to assure the cleanliness of his food. They told me not to even try to feed him a fresh orange, because there was no way to wash it enough that I would not transfer an invisible bug from peel to pulp. Then, when he was never nauseated, Wayne convinced himself that it was because I had worked so hard to feed him perfect, clean food.

Cancer has become to me a member of a class of things I cannot accept: like a stain on a white tablecloth, a smudge on the wall, a crack in the window through which I see the world, a wild growth in my husband's body. In my wish to rid my world of it, I have attacked the whole category. If I can clean out my closet, if only I can reach that spider web, I will create a world without evil.

So I feel. But it is not true, is it?

I have joined a grief support group, sponsored by

Hospice. Every other Monday I meet in their headquarters, forty-five minutes from my home, with a group of men and women who have lost their mates and are trying to work through the emotions and adjustments of this experience.

My family and friends know that I am not an effusive woman. I am not prone to express openly affection or dislike or anger or disappointment. I sometimes err by keeping to myself things I should say. Still, knowing somehow that I need to grieve and say it, I joined this group and attend faithfully.

In the group of twelve to fourteen men and women there are people for whom the loss is fresh and those who are two or three years ahead of us in the process we share; there are stoics and people who cannot talk without weeping. Some sob, some curse, some calmly say, "I'm lost." We take turns. The group just gives everybody time. We listen, we wait. No matter what anyone says, we accept it, we know it's true, we understand. We comfort one another.

Last Monday was a revelation to me. Something new and mysterious was going on in my life, and I confess that I drove to Hospice wondering why I had not been able to write lately. I had committed to doing an article, and then I couldn't. While someone waited for it, I struggled, unable to figure out where it was going or how to get three sensible sentences to follow one another toward some conclusion. There were existing articles I might read that would give me necessary information, but when I tried to read them, I became impatient. My brain seemed to lack energy to absorb facts. I jumped to something else without getting to the end of anything.

I found this a little frightening and suspected that I

was getting old very fast.

Then in the group, we were offered a chance to update the others, and when it was Jeanine's turn to tell what might be happening to her now, she said that she couldn't make the simplest decision. She stood in the closet for five minutes, her blue top in one hand, the red one in the other, unable to decide which to wear.

Our astute leader then asked if anyone else was having a similar experience, and I jumped in to confess, not that I can't decide what to put on in the morning or what to eat for breakfast, but that I am so distracted and feeble-minded that I can't express myself on paper or focus, even on a subject I really care about. I just wanted to know, is this part of the syndrome? Or am I losing my mind?

Suddenly half the people in the room wanted to assure me that they also could not concentrate. A woman widowed now two and a half years said she had not once read a book in all this time. Others said, "Me too." Joe said he used to work crossword puzzles, but now he can't. Then people started telling stories about lost keys and cell phones, unpaid bills, notes all over the house (intended to be reminders but ignored), work neglected, objects showing up in preposterous places. We began to laugh. We laughed until we wiped tears.

Our facilitator then advised us, "Unless a doctor tells you that there is clinical evidence, don't be afraid that this is about old age. Everybody experiences this kind of mental distraction when they are grieving."

I felt a weight slide right off my back and became quite confident that I am normal, with reason to hope I can still function like an intelligent person. I told the group, "The trip over was definitely worth it today."

The same man who two weeks before had said he wasn't sure that talking about it was helping, confessed, "I really needed that laugh."

Though I had never done such a thing before, my grandson Jeremy and his bride Michaela insisted upon my conducting their wedding ceremony. More charmed by their gentle insistence than truly persuaded, I summoned all my courage and advice from the experienced, and did it.

When I got home after the weekend of the wedding, feeling so honored and so glad about accepting this duty, having done it well and then danced with my happy family, when I was back home in my empty house, the party suddenly over, I unpacked my suitcase in haste, washed my clothes, put everything where it belonged, then sat down to write a list for tomorrow, a list to make the future seem real, and suddenly, without warning, felt myself falling into a black and blacker hole.

Falling is such a helpless feeling. Gravity is suddenly an enemy, jerking you down, and you know, but cannot resist. It was like that. Like falling off a ladder, the ground flying up to meet me, the truth slamming into my head.

Wayne missed Jeremy's wedding.

He should have stood where I stood and said the sacred words. It was his right. He was Grandpa, the minister. He was robbed. I was blessed because he was robbed.

No, I was robbed too, because I had this dear memory, and now I could not tell him. I could not explain to him how beautiful it was. I had to go to bed with this secret joy, this unexpected, detestable sorrow.

The next week in the grief support group, our leader remembered that I was to officiate my grandson's wedding, and, expectantly, she called on me to share.

I told the story, all of it. That I had done well. That everyone had been happy, I had been happy. That then I had come home and fallen into a dark and ugly place. That I had been fighting with myself ever since about my right to my own life. My head knows, I said, that since I am still here, I must have a right to live. I think I am supposed to do things that give me pleasure, things that fulfill my purpose. I have to claim my own life. I am supposed to dance sometimes.

A woman gasped while I was talking. I thought she was scandalized when I said I have a right to my own life, but then she said, "That is profound."

Others agreed that they had had experiences like mine. A reluctance to be joyful. An unwillingness to eat the favorite food of the deceased, to go where she wanted to go without her.

I came home after that conversation, feeling that I had made progress, not because anything that was broken before was now fixed, but just because I had managed to tell the truth, to say aloud what goes on inside of me. Honesty requires admitting how hard it is.

One woman in our group feels angry. Her husband died like mine did; he had stage four cancer, but his heart stopped, so he was gone suddenly. And she is so much younger than I am. She wiped her tears and said, "Damn you!" That was honest. She feels abandoned in the middle of her life.

But I am not angry. Not at God. Not at Wayne. They both gave me freedom, always. Wayne expected me to have a life of my own. When I was packing my suitcase for a trip that he couldn't take, he would say, "I hope it's going to be a really special time for you." And when I came back, he wanted to know everything. For so many years, I could go and do my thing and come back and see him take vicarious pleasure in what I had done without him.

Now I discover this didn't prepare me to have just half of that. I want to see that pleasure on his face.

One moment the dead are conspicuous by their absence. The next they are looking over our shoulder.

This reality is like an itch I can't reach. It shows up while I am trying to make a decision, simple or complex. Recently, for instance, it complicated a thing already difficult. I got our house painted. It needed new paint badly. Wayne had known it for a long time without feeling able to do anything.

The hard part is that I changed the color. We had collaborated on the old color that was like freshly sawn wood, a color that saved the original blond lumber, something Wayne always wanted to do. Around the front door I often noticed that the grain of the wood still showed, with beautiful knots here and there.

But for its own protection I had to paint the house.

I went to the paint store, looked at those little colored strips of paper and at folders full of suggestions about which colors like each other. I chose several colors, bought samples, tried them on the corners of the house and selected finally a sage green.

So now my house is this subtle green, with dark brown trim around the roof lines and corner frames. And the inside of the front stoop is nearly white, so light and welcoming, with a shiny dark brown door.

I like it, but . . . It is so different from what we did together twenty years ago. I miss the way it was. I get scary feelings of regret.

But the green is nice. Green is better now, I think. It fits so comfortably against the background of trees. It is a modest color, not showy or self-conscious.

But does Wayne like it? I don't want him to be disappointed in what I've done. He loved the swirls and knots of those beautiful boards around the front door. I have covered them up.

But the entry is so welcoming now. Its mood is happy, and the shiny door is modern.

I wrote to my son Dwight and said, "I hope your dad likes it."

And he replied, "If you like it, he likes it, Mom, because that's all he cares about."

This morning I told June this little story. June has been a widow a couple of years longer than I. She said, "Isn't it crazy? They are not here for us, but they never leave us alone."

Once every week or two I go to the cemetery and

look down at the headstone and talk to my husband. I tell him what I have done since I was there last.

I ordered pellet fuel early because the price goes up in September. And I got the propane tank filled up too, so I am ready for winter.

Jim helped me gather up all the useless things we had lying around. Scrap lumber from the deck repairs, paint cans and plastic tubs, my crock pot that died, and I paid a couple of guys to load it all up and take it to the dump. Our place looks really nice. New paint and a clean back yard.

I made chicken soup and invited Anita to have lunch with me. It was just a little awkward, I tell him, because I am working a jigsaw puzzle on the dining table. It's a hard puzzle, by the way; I could use some help.

The new Music on the Divide season started with an orchestra in the amphitheater. I sat with Nancy and Eileen. You would have liked the trumpet solo.

Things like that. I like to give him an update on the family. Marissa has gone to Mexico to teach for a year. Dwight is remodeling their kitchen forever and Sylvia is really tired of making beans in the crock pot. Sam has been at McKinsey a whole year now and is expecting a raise soon.

I hang around a while, not wanting to forget anything I meant to say. Always I make a point of telling him that I am O.K., because I promised him that I would be O.K.

That reminds me to tell him I have started writing again and joined a little group. Three other women. We meet on the second Tuesday of the month at the library and critique one another's work.

Right then I realize how hard it will be to do something that big, like publishing another book, if he isn't cheering from the sidelines. But I don't mention it, maybe because I don't want to think about it yet.

Whether or not going to the cemetery to visit the dead is normal and sane I don't know. I only know I need to do it. It seems a courteous thing. Sometimes I sweep dust and minor debris off the stone and put flowers in the vase. Sometimes the scattered pine needles and bits of earth and empty vase seem to make an appropriate statement, like "this earth is just a tired, messed up place," and I leave them.

After a while I say goodbye and go back to my car, always newly bereft, but somehow satisfied.

One time it came clear to me what I had just done. I had organized my own head. I had faced the truth that all those things I told him about had happened while he was not here. All those things I reported doing, I did without him. Life had gone on, whether I wanted it to or not.

I am the one who needed to understand that.

It came to me this week in a kind of epiphany, and I am surprised now that it has taken me more than a year to realize something that should be obvious.

I had made myself a nice, though simple meal. As I sat down in my favorite chair in the living room with the plate on a tray in my lap, I noticed the bright colors, a browned piece of fish, a mound of barely cooked broccoli and some raw carrots. That seemed to trigger a little flashback in my head. Early in our marriage Wayne, seeing me hesitate about the arrangement of meat and potatoes and salad on his plate, seemed surprised and said, "You even thought about how it was going to look."

And in recent years he often remarked that his food was beautiful.

I began eating, and my mind just stepped nimbly from one thought to another, until I was imagining Wayne sitting here in the living room, thinking about me and eating alone. It would not be fish and vegetables on his plate. Probably pancakes or a grilled cheese sandwich. Or in the morning, oatmeal with chocolate chips on top, "brown sugar" he called them.

Wayne was so gregarious, so affectionate, so grateful to people who worked in kitchens and brought out things he liked, so happy to never even wonder what was for lunch.

He would be so lonely.

Once, only once in the past year, I sat at the dining table by myself, and that was because I was dressed to go out and afraid of dropping something on my white blouse. I usually ate too fast and went on to something else.

He was lonely enough in his life, while I studied a whole school year in Virginia, while I traveled to Egypt and Russia and the Far East on various work assignments, while I spent two weeks at a time in Lebanon, leaving him in Cyprus. He worried about me besides, not satisfied that I was safe.

Here in this big house, if I were gone, he would walk from room to room, looking for some hint of my presence.

For so many years in the mornings, always up before me, he would greet me in the living room with a small hug, saying, "Sit here. I will bring your coffee." How could he ever be himself again if he couldn't do that?

What would he do on a cold, foggy day like today when he could not work outside or go for a slow walk around the neighborhood? I'm afraid he would sit in that cluttered little office in front of his computer and look at all those old pictures of his parents and brothers and sister and coaches and teammates and wife, all gone.

I fear he would cry, turning back the covers to go to bed. And then he would have no one to rub his arthritic neck; no one to put lotion on his itchy back.

He would manage, I guess. He would go to the store and buy cooked chicken strips and those potatoes that he liked and I didn't. He would do his laundry eventually, work clothes and dress shirts, all together. He would spread the bed roughly, some days at least, thinking that how it looked was not really important. He would never get the pillow cases on properly.

He would sit on the couch reading and look up, saying, "Listen to this," then see my empty chair and remember that I was not coming back.

So I thought, and at this point I started to realize that I didn't want any of this for him, the way I didn't want him to hurt in his back and keep moving to a different chair or trying another pillow.

And I started to feel glad. It felt inappropriate and clumsy at first, like stubbing my toe on a stone and then, in pain, discovering the stone was something wonderful that I had lost. I was so glad. Glad that he didn't have to hear my head hit the wall as I fell backward. Glad he didn't ever have to stand on the front stoop and watch the tail lights of the hearse disappear, carrying my body away. How wonderful that he would never need to come to the cemetery to talk to me.

I have been at times resentful, I admit, that in spite of living cleanly all his life, even though he was muscled and strong, without consideration for the fact that he deliberately tried to make the world better, he was struck down by a heart attack, all those years ago, at the age of sixty-two. I especially noticed how unfair it was when that neighbor who sat on the porch smoking and drinking beer all day down in the next block just kept enjoying the sunshine day after day. Or so it seemed.

And then, after all that Wayne did, even with a crippled heart, and though he seemed to deserve in every way to be healthy and happy, he was assaulted by a nasty, mean cancer.

But finally I understand what he gained.

Couples almost never die together. One dies and leaves the other. And I somehow, without intending, have spared him the pain of being the other.

By out-living him, I have given him a gift. It is costing me a lot, but given the choice, this is what I would have wanted.

My heart is puzzled, drenched with the blessing of this sorrow, that I survived him.

I Will Live in My House

Less than a month after the death of my husband people were asking me, "What will you do?"

They didn't ask this just because I was a widow, but because I was an eighty-eight year old widow. An old woman with osteoporosis and a big house with stairs and a big yard and offspring scattered from the northwest to the southeast. A stooped old woman who was feeling stunned and numb. And that's what people always wonder about stooped and stunned old women left alone. What will they do?

Predictably stubborn, I said, "I will carry on."

Six months earlier I had dropped everything else I cared about to do one thing: take care of Wayne, my husband of sixty-three years who now had pancreatic cancer besides his fragile heart. There was no question in my mind that one day I would "carry on," that is, go back to the rest of my life. I would write, teach my Wednesday Bible study, go to my book club meetings ready to discuss the relevant book, lunch out with the Red Hatters, keep house, host family and friends on holidays, etc., etc.

The first thing my words meant was simply that I would continue to live in my house. And my house was here.

I admit that I did not totally understand yet the ways it had changed. Not the floor plan, not the colors of the walls, not the stairs or the lamps, not the way the moonlight makes bright rectangles on the bedroom wall, but something deeper and more subtle that both hurts and consoles me.

I am aware that this is one way that old people become problems. They refuse to budge from their houses no matter how many responsible offspring worry about them. They get attached to their places.

Often the younger people in a family have a hard time understanding why the old, their parents, are so attached to home. They can see all the advantages to moving to some place smaller and easier to take care of, or someplace where we will be safer and cared for. But in the mind of the elderly that "someplace" is a strange place where we don't know anybody, and the whole pattern of living is different. And this is being suggested just when we need our friends and familiar activities the most.

My family, I believe, is more understanding than many, more understanding than I was of my mother, because they all know the meaning of this house, they all participated in building it. Doing this was a bonding experience and gave them appreciation for every room, every detail. They can look at the floor, for instance, and remember the teamwork involved in putting it down.

Jim would say, with the big mechanical measuring tape in his hand, we need a board four feet one and a half inches, and I with my little cloth sewing tape would choose from the stack, the piece that was closest by slightly more. Wayne would take that piece down the stairs to his shop and cut it, and make the little groove needed in the end to fit it to the next piece, and when he brought it back Dwight would put it into its place. So the floor grew the way a puzzle becomes a picture, piece by piece. It took a team of four Fullers to make this happen.

The last room to get a floor was the music room upstairs; we were down to scraps of material, an assortment of types in varying colors, and Jim designed the most beautiful floor in the house, beginning with a four and three-quarter inch square, composed of four triangular pieces. The square grows magically, by the imaginative placement of pieces in varying lengths, until it is approximately fifteen inches, and then four big triangles, jagged on the sides like step pyramids grow, spreading out toward the walls, in a geometrical pattern for which I need mathematical terms not in my vocabulary. You don't get wonders like that in houses built in bunches to make money. You don't get such details in a house built in a hurry to get shelter. And you don't get the memory if you just buy a house.

So my family understands. My leaving the house might be as hard for them as it is for me.

And leaving houses is something I have grown weary of doing.

Between 1963 and 1995 I lived in eighteen houses in five countries. Actually seventeen houses and one luxury hotel where we were war refugees in Tehran (strange as that may seem now). I wrote a memoir that covers events of only eight of those thirty-two years, and I called it, *In Borrowed Houses*.

In some of those residences we had nothing of our own except what was in our suitcases, having been separated for long periods of time from our possessions. That's why we wound up finally with so many sets of cheap sheets and towels and skillets.

I can honestly say that I have been adaptable. I managed. I did not complain, because there was no one to blame. I was never giddy about it, but I was grateful. I believed that wherever we put our family was home.

When we retired from this accidentally nomadic life, we had no place to go except a wooded lot in the foothills of the Sierras. Our children had all come to the States ahead of us, each to a different state, unable to answer when people asked where they were from.

Planning this house was a family affair. People submitted pictures and drawings of floor plans. It had to be big enough for everyone to come at once. All ideas, practical or visionary, were considered.

We built it in stages. Everybody worked. Sons, daughters, in-laws, girlfriends, neighbors, children. Some college kids, who dropped by to spend the weekend, were put to work in exchange for getting their names in the stew pot. We have a picture of our daughter Jan on a back hoe and a snap of three little boys carrying one long board on their shoulders.

Wayne bought one gigantic oak tree that had been drying for about five years, and out of that tree he made baseboards, stair risers, door frames, railings, and trim, for all three levels of this house. And oh yes, the lovely sloped ceiling over the living room and loft. He never tired of telling the story.

Unique decorative details remind me always of how he thought ahead, bringing, in a crate from the Middle

East, strips of tiny carved posts bought on the street in Cairo, just because he liked them. Imaginatively placed in my kitchen and bathroom, they make these rooms unlike any others in the world.

My job, besides feeding the hungry workers, was shopping for building materials. I found every tile store within fifty miles, decided the color scheme, brought home samples and chose the tiles and paint. We painted the dining room three times before we got the exact shade of blue-green that I wanted. (It had to enhance Jan's needlepoint angel, memento of a significant family event. Seeing that angel, you are supposed to think, Frances. The baby in her arms is Samuel, whom I adopted after he was found, newborn, in a damaged and abandoned building. This is a novel way, I admit, to get a grandson.)

So it happens that the skill and vision of my whole creative family are visible in these rooms. My children's finger prints and Wayne's personality are everywhere.

I am full of excuses and acting like my situation is different from that of any other elderly woman wanting to stay in her house, but of course, it is different only in the details. Everybody has her own reasons, just as significant as mine, most with the same result.

I used to think that I would be afraid living in such a big house alone. But I am not. I know the sound the refrigerator makes, dumping a batch of ice cubes. I recognize the little pops that the window sills and floor boards make in the middle of the night. No one is breaking into the house; the temperature is just changing, and the house is contracting or expanding. This house is a living thing, a friend of mine. Like a child, perhaps, I find comfort in the familiar and in the meanings beyond wood and paint, deeper than shelter from the rain.

The day I move from here will feel like the day that the youngest member of this family lost her security blanket, a ragged scrap of flannel, and we had to come home from Six Flags without it. Vanessa's heartbreak created a contagious tsunami of tears.

In exchange for this kind of empathy, I now make a promise, a compromise. When I can no longer manage, I will admit it. I can welcome someone to live with me here, if that solves a problem. Otherwise I have to leave. This lovely place is not my life but just another borrowed house. Saying this now, though only half believing it, I am making it possible for others to remind me, if necessary. If I need to, if others need me to, I will leave the house. I intend to actually try to do it cheerfully, though not without sorrow.

Foremost among my reasons is the conviction that it would not be fair to let my family be so worried that they have to come and announce that I am moving and pack me off against my will. Nobody wants to do that, and if I am in my right mind, I will not let this happen.

If necessary, someone can remind me that I said this.

I Will Mop the Kitchen Floor

Years ago we had some neighbors; well, they were sort of neighbors. They lived several doors from us, but we had never known them or been to their house, having been told that they did not welcome visitors. In fact, a generous neighbor once delivered a casserole to that house, considering it just a gesture of good will, and was told at the door, "We don't like people to come to our house without calling first."

They were artists, we heard, one a painter, the other a sculptor. Because they lived like hermits, we barely noticed when they passed away.

He was gone first, then two or three years dragged by, and we hardly glimpsed or heard of this woman until we saw a bit of activity, a strange car or two there, and the news went around the neighborhood that she had died.

After that for a long while, the house just sat there, deserted. A couple of vehicles stood in the yard, outside the garage, as though there was no room for them inside. Since our son Dwight was at the time looking for a house to buy and interested in being near us, we were curious. Was the house available for purchase?

We asked people who had been here longer, seeking information about who might have inherited the house. We were told there were a son and a daughter who did not speak to one another. They lived elsewhere and deliberately never came together to visit their parents. How they could agree on what to do with the house was a big question. In fact, all the old couple's possessions were still there, because if one of the siblings took anything and the other came and missed it, there would be a lawsuit.

Though it felt sneaky and impolite, we resorted to looking in the windows like peeping toms to get an idea of the layout of the house. What we saw was barely believable. The rooms were full, stuffed, crowded, with furniture, crude plaster figures, canvases splashed with paint, many in frames, leaning against the walls. There was little space to walk. The carpeted stairway, visible through a bit of glass in the front door was littered with orange peelings and unidentifiable garbage.

At a family gathering of our own, Dwight related to his brothers and sisters what we had seen, and as everyone listened, some responded with exclamations and shocked facial expressions. I tried to explain. I said, "Well, it is a dysfunctional situation. The house is a picture of the family."

Even then, everybody was partly amused along with partly horrified, until I added, "Like every house."

I had not intended to push the pause button on this conversation, but smiles vanished. Silence hung for a long moment over our dinner table. Then someone said quietly, "I think I need to go home and clean up my house."

And another added, "I'm going to start in the back of my closet." Nobody even laughed.

Sometimes we need an extreme example to make us see what's normal. When a house is like the one described above, it means something: dysfunction, depression, mental illness, physical handicaps, lack of awareness . . .

In my house, in my thinking, the floor is a barometer, especially the kitchen, and everybody knows it.

My mother was an excellent housekeeper. She didn't know how to decorate, nor did she have the money to do it, but her house was clean, top to bottom, in the middle and in the corners, inside and out. When she was old and failing and I went to visit, I checked behind the potty, under the kitchen sink, the window sills, because dirt anywhere would mean that Mother was losing it, physically, mentally or emotionally.

The time came when she couldn't do the work, but she had help, and she had all of her brains. In her head she kept the work schedules for people who were coming; she was ready to pass out assignments: changing the sheets, scrubbing the bathroom, wiping out the cupboards, running errands. She was sitting in her chair rubbing swollen arthritic knees but her house was clean.

I am not my mother. I can and will do all sorts of things she never dreamed of doing. In spite of her numerous instructions in how-to and in the face of her example, I am likely to read, write, travel, teach, study, argue, play Scrabble and watch basketball while my house disintegrates around me. Except for the kitchen floor.

I think this started long ago when Wayne knocked down the wall of our front porch to add several feet to a dark and cramped kitchen. This called for a complete paint job and a new floor. Linoleum was the trend, at least the one we could afford, and we chose yellow. Not solid yellow; there was some kind of subtle pattern that I have forgotten. To our surprise the white ceiling reflected the glow of the floor, and it was as though the sun shone all day in that kitchen.

There may have been something inappropriate about the way I loved that yellow floor. I protected and pampered it. Every night, after the dishes were done, I mopped it.

This became a habit, even a bit of an obsession. One of my daughters-in-law was dismayed when she learned that I mopped my kitchen floor every night. She didn't yet understand that it didn't mean a thing about my overall standard, or that I pay little attention to other people's floors.

Vowing to mop the kitchen floor is easy, because it is my thing, but now there is another reason that I must do it. Remembering what I did, I suspect that my children will be looking for little signs that I can't be trusted here. And they know me; the kitchen floor will be a dead giveaway.

I Will Learn To Ask for Help

Last summer just a few days before my husband died, we got a letter from the company that insures our property. The letter stated that our insurance would be canceled on a certain date, two months in the future, for failure to comply with fire safety rules. I went to the company's local agent immediately to tell him that my husband was terminally ill, and I did not want him to know about this. The news would be devastating, because he could do nothing.

It happens that our son Dwight is a school teacher, so he gets a long summer vacation. He intended to use the time to remodel his kitchen. Instead, a few days after Wayne's memorial, he started coming to my house daily to cut down trees deemed to be too close to the house, strip the limbs and pile them up, cut the trees into rounds and split the rounds. Day after day in the hot sun, he worked. I hired a helper who gave us a few hours; a friend came for several days. We had a professional tree cutter for one day to fell the really difficult ones. A son-in-law came up from Southern California. But through it all Dwight was here, dirty and sunburned, working so tirelessly that the other men named him "The Machine."

When the job was finished it was almost time to go back to school. I got to keep my insurance, but Dwight never touched his kitchen. And I had lost more than seventy trees, among them five majestic giants that had protected my house from the heat of afternoon.

This was not a stupendous start to my independent life alone.

Needs arrive more often than I would have imagined. I have begun to suspect that little disasters are lined up waiting to attack old ladies who are alone. Like those two exhaust fans, mounted in the walls, that had cooled the house these twenty summers, choosing to die, both of them, in the midst of an insufferable heat wave. Like that puddle of water on the beautiful hardwood floor of my dining room on a Saturday night at the end of an already long and strenuous day. Walking through the dimly lighted room on my way to the phone, I felt the splash, and turned on a light. It was not a spill but a pond, overflow from the lake in my kitchen.

How? Where? Flinging open the freezer door of the refrigerator I saw the ice cube basket full of water and spilling over.

Sloshing across the room, I grabbed a stack of towels and began throwing them down, picking them up and wringing them out into my mop bucket, still sitting there because I had cleaned the floor earlier before going out for dinner. For maybe fifteen minutes I was bent over, sopping up water, dumping the pail and starting over.

Finally, with an aching back, I called my son Jim who lives two hours from here to ask him, "How do I stop water from flowing into my ice maker?" He told me the bad news that I had to pull the refrigerator out of its pocket between the broom closet and the oven and close the valve on the wall. "It's not hard," he said, "but you will need help."

I called my neighbor. For the third time that day I called Mike whose wife had a miserable cold and answered the other two times when I wanted to borrow a dolly.

"I feel like a pest," I began. Mike comforted me by acting like himself, saying, "You are a pest."

He came, his hair still wet from a bedtime shower, and Jim was right. Moving that refrigerator out of its space is not terribly hard if you are six feet four with arms long enough to hug a slippery monster. And turning off the valve is easy if your hands are muscled from gripping wrenches and hammers.

Of course there was a lot of dirt back there behind the fridge, years' worth of dirt, now wet, so after I cleaned it up and Mike put the malfunctioning monster back in its place and went home, I mopped up our tracks, which made the third time that day that I mopped the kitchen floor.

I went to bed hurting inside and out, my old muscles too tired to relax, and my old-lady pride tested.

When you are a woman and eighty-eight, the practicalities of life can pile up and test your confidence that living alone in a big house is doable. Without family, neighbors, friends it is not doable, and all those people are sincere when they say, just ask. Before he left, Mike assured me that I was not a pest.

What I've learned is that some people like it when you tell them what you need. They feel special or useful or, I don't know, maybe important. And important they are.

Within one week all these things happened to me: First I woke with an aching head and a sore throat. Then I woke with a two-day-old headache, a worsening sore throat and one red eye leaking junk. The third day I still had all of that with work to do before breakfast, and an apparently dead computer. The report I had written the night before was due in someone else's mailbox and I couldn't send it. And my folder of tax information was due at the tax lady's office, and I had not received my annual earnings report from Social Security.

When I am sick I do not lose heart; I usually get well. But a lifeless computer is cause for panic; I count the weeks since I backed up my documents; the specter of catastrophic loss looms. To save myself from my own wild imagination, I quickly called my friends the Fishers, looking for their young genius named Ben.

That day I got Ben's cheerful father, Greg, and cried on his shoulder about the disaster, including my unwillingness to have Ben come here and catch a cold and pink eye. Greg said, "How about this? I run over, grab your computer at the door and bring it to Ben. When he has it fixed, I will bring it back."

According to me, it is twenty minutes from their door to mine; in fifteen he was here. When I saw my computer go out the door I thought to call someone and apologize that my report would not make it to the council meeting, but instead I drank coffee and ate some toast and then Greg was back. I turned on the computer. It booted! I asked what Ben did. He said, "You know; he just passed his magic fingers over it."

Though it was a holiday, my sweet eye doctor met me at her otherwise deserted office building, looked in my red and painful eye, told me I was right that I had pink eye, but also it couldn't get well with an eyelash scratching it. In seconds she plucked out the errant eyelash and gave me drops to apply three times a day, enabling me to go on with my suspenseful life.

On an ordinary Tuesday I took most, not all my relevant information to Heather, my tax lady, so she could tell the government that I don't make enough money to support them and me too. This little trip could be an odious necessity, but it happens that my "tax lady" is also the "hat lady." She would be wearing a hat and one could never predict its character: gorgeous with wide brim and flowers or an old fashioned bonnet tied under her chin. But I was short that one document. I explained to Heather that I suspected a mix-up about my address. She listened, sitting there wearing her big smile and a white bunny beanie with ears as I said, "I felt I needed to go over to the Social Security office, take a number and sit there six hours until I could talk to somebody about this, but I didn't think I could hold my achy head up so long."

She said, "Don't worry, I'll just use your bank records and calculate what we need to know, and when you come back we will sit at the computer together and set up an online account with you at Social Security, and if they have your address wrong, we will change it."

That sounded like a fun and simple solution to a boring problem and I felt so grateful, but I said, "That's service beyond your duty," and the best tax/hat lady on earth said, "You know, if you have a skill and you don't share it, it's not even fun."

The truth is that most weeks I survive because other people have skills that I don't and some of these people are amazingly helpful and generous.

One of my problems is that my hearing is very bad, so I have spent a lot of money for a hearing aid, and now I am going to wear it. I feel the need to say that only because I know people who hate their hearing aids. My husband never learned to appreciate his. A hearing aid specialist explained to me that Wayne probably had become accustomed to a quiet world and subconsciously liked it. The hearing aid created an obnoxious squawk in his ears.

We had some hilarious conversations, Wayne and I, but they were often not funny while in progress. He made my life so much more difficult by not bothering to put the help we had paid for into his ears. Once I burst into tears and raised my voice, "Where is your four thousand dollar hearing aid?" He then put those expensive little gadgets where they belonged and I felt ashamed for shouting at him.

Though it sometimes made me angry, I knew the loss was really his. He loved small children but could no longer hear their little soprano voices. No alarm could reach him when he had to wake for an early morning event. And in our own family, he was often left out of conversations.

I feel certain that if he had understood how much energy it took to say everything four times, he would have learned to wear his hearing aid. But he had so many miseries to deal with—painful osteoarthritis in his neck, itches on his back, bouts of arrhythmia. All of this and then discomfort in his abdomen and the news that he was dying. And he could not bear to let his problems be a hardship for me. He once stood near the door of our house with tears in his eyes, while I walked across the yard pushing a wheelbarrow with a few sticks of wood in it. I thought it was rather fun, but he felt that bringing wood into the house was his job and letting me do it was abusive. So, because of his basic kindness I accepted his deafness. Most of the time.

Hearing aids cost a lot of money. Every year they get better and more expensive. The man who sold me mine told me to put them in my ears every morning, immediately when I get up, even if I am alone and not trying to hear anything. In fact, I do hear a lot of things that are simply absent if I don't wear them. When I walk out to the street to get the mail, a blue jay screeches at me. And I tell him, "O.K. it's your tree, but it's my yard." Before I got my hearing aid I did not have conversations with birds.

Conversing with birds made me notice that I can't think of a tree as mine. This place was a forest. I am the invader. See, wearing my hearing aid is a way of living more. It shows appreciation for the opportunity. If I am alive, shouldn't I tune in to the world?

And if I am going to be with other people, shouldn't I relate? Yesterday I went to my book club meeting and not once did I have to ask anyone to repeat what she had said. That made the meeting easier for me and everyone else. I picked up other people's insights into the novel we had read.

Wearing my hearing aid is a way of admitting my limitation and getting help.

The fact is that I don't always have to ask for help. More than that, I really dislike asking for help. So sometimes I find ways to overcome my weaknesses.

In the summer I bought a big watermelon. I have an inordinate love for watermelon and, having grown up in Arkansas, I know a really good watermelon from a passable watermelon. In other words, I'm picky. Knowing that the heart of the melon is the best part, I want a big one. I rarely meet a small melon that satisfies me and tend to buy the biggest one I can wrestle into my shopping cart.

But last summer I was alone already and longing for a watermelon. When I took my purse out of the upper part of the basket so I could balance there the melon I had chosen, I had a vague feeling that I was setting myself up for a problem. Then when I half dropped it into the trunk of my car, I realized that lifting it out was not a good idea for a woman with osteoporosis who had already broken her back once by mishandling a heavy object.

When I got home, I created a space in my refrigerator for the melon but knew that I could not put it there myself. I would simply have to leave it in the car until someone came to help me. But my mouth was already watering in expectation of the crunchy sweet heart of that melon. I stood staring at it, and I thought, "What would Wayne Fuller do?"

One of my husband's often repeated slogans was, "Use your head to save your back."

A light bulb blinked on. Yes, I should try that. I put a big piece of plastic in the trunk and rolled the melon onto it. I brought my best sharp knife, and I whacked that melon across its middle, right through its delicious red heart. Each half was manageable, so I covered the cut surfaces with plastic and carried each piece to the refrigerator.

For a week I enjoyed eating that thing, the flavor enhanced by the fun of cutting it in the trunk of the car.

This is all to say that every little problem I can solve for myself will save my helpers a bit of bother and make me feel smart and independent. So, I usually try first before I ask for help.

I Will Be Responsible for Loneliness

There is a song that says, "Rainy days and Mondays always get me down." This morning I think, What if it is both rainy and Monday, and what if you are a widow with a nasty cold and no appointments and no expectation of seeing another human today?

The mailman will come in his little jeep with the steering wheel on the right, but I can't expect to see him when he puts a couple of bills in my box by the road. The box is a hundred and twenty steps from my door; well, maybe a hundred and ten manly strides. We counted. Again and again we counted, because we had to prove to the property insurance company that the trees out there were more than a hundred feet from the house. That's how we saved their lives.

Anita will walk her little dog, but if I happen to go out for the mail just when she is in front of my house, that will be a twice-a-month coincidence.

I thought all of this first thing in the morning, still lying in bed, and then I decided that today, this 12th of February, I don't mind. I will study, write, eat what is readily available and make gagging noises when coughing, without troubling anyone else. Maybe I will organize the cluttered dressing table in my bathroom. Maybe not.

No one, not my neighbor, the mailman, my daughter who is 2,718.9 miles away, or any of the significant people in my life are responsible—for the weather, the mail in my box, my dressing table, my health, my loneliness. It is not their problem.

But this is not every day. Today I am braver than some days.

Lately I have noticed an emotional neediness that does not feel natural. Lonely on Sunday afternoons and at the end of a normal day, I grab my phone or my tablet, looking for a text from someone. Sometimes I keep it near me while I try to read a book or watch a game on television, thinking that I have a big family; surely someone is thinking of me, remembering that I am here, needing to talk to someone.

But, what do I want to talk about? Do I have something to tell? Not really. I just want to hear their story. How is your job going? What did you learn today? Did you see the ball game? When are you coming? To keep them going, I make up trivial questions.

The real problem is my neediness. They are busy. They have a lot of people besides me in their lives. They can't know that none of the other twenty-four members of the family are talking to me tonight. They don't have any big news or I would hear it. They are in a meeting. They have to study for tomorrow. They are grading student papers. They are practicing for the Easter musical. They are out with friends and it would be rude to answer a text right now. In other words, they have a life. Good for them. Be proud. Take care of yourself for goodness sake.

OK, I am admitting that I have come to a bumpy stretch in the road. I never expected this. I am Miss Independence. When I put this promise in my outline, I was boasting, so sure was I that I would not be lonely. I have always been good at being alone. I always needed to read, write, study, prepare a speech and especially to process my own reactions to an experience or an idea.

Isn't a part of every human underground, out of sight, like the roots of a tree? Yes, but the branches and the leaves reach up and out for air and sun, and even I am not built to be a hermit. Sometimes aloneness becomes too much, like when it stretches for days of cooking, eating, praying, mopping the floor, hearing and dealing with the news of the world, my own sickness and a holiday that used to mean hugs and flowers.

I was thinking about those admirable friends of mine who never married. There were several in the Middle East with us, women who were single, facing the strange culture, the social restrictions of living singly in the Arab world, far from family, with no life companion.

They were not, to be sure, a homogeneous group. Their differences were very noticeable. There were some who considered themselves victims of the family system. They were lonely and blamed other people for ignoring them, for being insensitive, for not including them. They didn't want to be alone; neither did they like being assigned a housemate, as though it didn't matter who they lived with. They were right, actually, about most of this.

But then there were others, women like Nancie Wingo, whom I called "the sunshine of the Lebanon mission." If she had a problem, she made light of it, in a self-deprecating way, as though it were all because she made some mistake or had a silly attitude. She thought we married women were the ones who had it rough, marveling that we could raise children in a foreign culture, cook for a family, learn the language and still deal with a husband. How did we ever do it?

She didn't even have time to be lonely, because everybody wanted her. Inviting her was a daunting thing, because one had to wait. Her calendar was full. She might have filled it herself by inviting people to her apartment. And her apartment was itself a pleasant place, simple and tasteful, modest and artistic, and dinner would be an interesting surprise.

Knowing people like Nancie made me put in my list of promises this one, that I would be responsible for my own loneliness. I did not intend to ever really need this. But, then, though I was sort of expecting to be an old lady, I had forgotten one of the given principles of life and was not expecting to be an old lady alone.

I was spoiled and a little bit ignorant. I didn't know how different the World Series was if you watch it alone. I didn't realize how often I wanted another opinion or how useless it was to ask the empty room a question.

But I do have resources. Sometimes I think of Nancie. She must have been in this situation a thousand times. What would she do?

She would make herself a cup of tea and phone someone to share it with, saying she was thinking of them.

At the sound of her voice the sun would come out in somebody else's house and discouragement flee with its tail between its legs.

If loneliness or any kind of complaint came up in the conversation she would agree and with her ironic gaiety turn the problem into just a humorous part of the craziness of life.

Suddenly today I remembered Cynthia at the age of five. This funny and delightful child, my youngest, had other less acceptable traits. One day I sent her to her room for some offense; it must been particularly egregious, because I gave her a long sentence. An hour is an eternity when one is five.

In the peace that descended, I sat at the kitchen table studying for the next day's Arabic lesson. After a while, the quiet began to sound suspicious. Tim was not playing the piano. The little boys were not in the back yard making truck noises.

Looking for Jan who had simply disappeared, I walked down the hall, as far as Cynthia's room where I found all five, sitting on Cynthia's pillows, drinking imaginary tea from Cynthia's toy cups, under a tent constructed of the spread and blankets from Cynthia's bed. She had positioned her tent so that the door opened into the hall, and she had invited in anyone who walked by. I too was invited.

What could I say? She had stayed in her room as instructed. No rules had been broken. I confess that I felt a little outsmarted.

Right now I see her wisdom. She took responsibility for her own loneliness. She found a way to be hospitable.

Learning from My Friends

We were in Roanoke, my daughter Jan and I with her best friend Jan Therien, sometimes called "Jan T" in our family, to avoid confusion. High on our list of things to do that weekend was visiting our mutual friend Gyn, who had fallen several times and was now in a care facility.

A little smaller than I remembered but still bouncy and bright, Gyn glowed with excitement in face and voice when she saw us, turning loose of her walker to hug each of us. Because there were only two chairs in the room, she insisted that Jan T and I take them. She sat with my Jan on the foot of the bed with no support for her back. To get there she took two wobbly, lopsided steps and bounced onto the foot of the bed.

She chattered and joked and glowed; I have to say "glowed." Though her face was pale it was shining. Her hair, short, thin and white was brushed straight backward adding to an appearance of surprise. She seemed so excited to see us.

The room itself was somehow drab, the walls gray, the comforter on the bed just a darker shade. Objects—the chairs, two large pictures on the wall, the newspaper on the floor, the lamp by the bed—all seemed scattered thoughtlessly.

Jan got up from the bed to peek through slats of the blinds and said, "Gyn, you have a WONDERFUL view of the mountains!" But the blind stayed closed.

Gyn talked brightly about politics, a coming election, friends, church (she had not felt like going in a long time).

Asked how long she had been here in this care facility, she said quickly, "One week, and I'm leaving soon."

Someone had told her, she said, that she could not drive her car anymore, but she did not know why he would say that. She knew she was a good driver.

"It's parked right out there," she said, pointing toward the window. "I pestered Jimmy 'til he brought it. I can see it when I look out."

"But Gyn," someone said, "we can't let you fall again."

"I won't fall. I just made a mistake that time I stepped on the ice. I saw the ice, but I thought I could go far enough to get my paper. I wanted my paper! They were supposed to put it in my carport, but there it was out on the lawn, and I need my paper in the morning."

Me too, I thought. I want my paper in the morning, enough to run some risks.

We all knew what happened. She had cracked her head hard and since then had often been confused, sometimes irrational. This knowledge seemed to sit in the room with us, carefully unstated.

I tried to chase it away by telling her that I had used her fruitcake recipe several times, and then she and I took turns, laughing all the while, trying to describe how hard it is to stir all those fruits and nuts into the dough.

"Aren't you clever?" she said when I described how I had found a way to mix it in a large flat pan to spread out the weight.

A sudden loud voice startled all of us. "Virginia, are you coming for the music?"

Gyn, looking up at the ceiling, did not understand. Again the voice.

"No," she said. "I have guests."

"They can come, too."

Ignoring that, she said to us, "It's some guy with a banjo."

Jan T said, "That thing is loud enough to jar your nerves."

"Oh, the first time I heard it, it woke me up in the morning, saying, 'Virginia!' and I'm wondering, who is Virginia."

"They woke you up?"

"The first morning I was here, to ask if I was coming for breakfast."

I said, "I never knew your name was Virginia."

"Well, I almost forgot it myself."

It was a happy visit. She was so glad we came. And sure, apparently, that she would not be there long.

In the parking lot, the two Jans told one another.

"She will not be going home." That fall on the ice was the worst, but she had fallen numerous times, they said.

I am trying to prepare myself for being in such a room, all day, all night. Down the hall at a desk will be people with the right and responsibility to wake me and ask if I am coming to breakfast. I must wake whether or not I wish. And if not, what will I eat?

I must plan. I must bring dear objects from home. I must have a rocking chair. My cross-stitch angel on the wall. A Hammoui painting. My little children's faces. And those of my wonderful, amazing grandchildren, my hope for the world.

I must have a bookshelf. Is there a library? If there is not a library with real literature, how will I live there?

"Do you see her car?" I asked.

"There it is. Right there. But you can be sure she doesn't have the key."

"No, Jimmy wouldn't give her the key."

I have to make it a place to live, not a place to die.

I have lived in so many borrowed houses. It will be just one more.

People who are close enough will pop in for visits. When they go I will smile. I will thank them.

I am in dread, a dread I never expected. A dread of not being able to make the decision myself, imposing it on my children, fighting them all the way.

Dread of the loneliness that descends when visitors leave.

When Wayne and I visited our friend Ruth in the assisted care facility, she obviously didn't know who we were. But neither did we know the people she thought we were, so in the conversation that happened we were even.

Sitting in the recliner beside her bed, perfectly made with a red spread, she looked like someone prepared and waiting for visitors. Even in her robe, she seemed dressed up. Her nails were polished, her red hair orderly, her lipstick flawless.

She stroked gently the small stuffed dog on her lap and told us his name. She boasted that he was always well behaved and never bothered her visitors.

Even so, she appeared to be engaged and alert.

When we asked if she liked the place, she said, "Oh, yes. They love me here. Everybody just treats me like a queen."

She told us that Mary was going to come and take her out to lunch. Mary has told me that her mother doesn't even know her.

"I hope she'll take me shopping," Ruth said, "because I really need some shoes." Her shoes were just disappearing. Someone was stealing them. She left her red high heels right here by the bed one night and in the morning they were gone; she couldn't understand who was stealing from her because all the people seemed so nice and they really loved her.

That made me notice her feet. She was wearing glittery slippers with a heel and a circle of faux fur around her instep. And below her robe, black slacks fell around her ankles. She could take off that robe and go to the dining hall looking like she had stepped out of Vogue-for-the-Elderly.

We told her that everyone in the church was missing her. She said she was going to surprise us sometime and show up.

I thought that she could not surprise me. I could visualize it. She would come wearing a classy suit in a bright color, with shoes, purse and jewelry coordinated.

Full of chatter, she began to tell us stories about her first-graders. We knew she had been a teacher for many years, but she had been retired for probably twenty-five.

She told us that her class came to visit her there in her room. They were so cute. One little boy didn't want to leave when the others did. He had told her, "I want to sleep here with you on this red bedspread." She had been obliged to let him. He was so sweet and she had invited him to come again.

That little dog, though, could be a problem at night. Sometimes he pushed her out of bed. She loved him anyway, she said, and stroked him around the ears.

Twice while we were there her eyes focused on the middle distance somewhere behind us, and she said, "There he is again. Every day I see this man's face. I don't know who he is."

We looked over our shoulders at nothing but a wall.

When we left, we promised to come again. But it was the last time we saw her.

Remembering, I ask myself who was happy during that hour we spent with Ruth, and the answer is clear. Ruth was happy. Except in that moment when the face she didn't know appeared on the wall. Except that her red high heels disappeared in the night.

She was happy. But I don't want to be there in her chair, petting my stuffed dog. I don't want my friend in the other chair to notice that I am clueless and happy.

Pride makes me say that now, but pride will not be the issue when I don't know the truth.

I suppose that what I must acknowledge is that Ruth was not responsible for the shrinking of her brain, and I do not have total control over mine. I read and write and work crosswords and study and teach and sometimes I don't find the word I need or I happen on an old friend in the grocery and can't say her name.

And I worry sometimes about who I will be when my faculties have eroded. Will I be pleasant to the stranger who knows me and cares enough to come?

I hope so. Fear is getting me nowhere.

I need to remember John.

Long into his nineties, he drove a big car. He had to have that car, because every day he drove nineteen miles of twisty mountain road and several more of city streets and went to the rest home to visit his wife. For twenty years he had done that; for the last ten she had not known him most of the time.

But now and then, she did. He lived for those rare moments when he walked into the room, and she said, "Well, there's Johnny!" It had not happened now for a couple of years.

Occasionally I spoke in the church, when the pastor was away and the official lay speaker was not available. It had been a month or more since I had done that when John said to me, "That sermon you preached, about Jesus in the book of Hebrews. You gave me a lot to think about. I'm still working on it."

He was 98. Honestly. I would bet my last dollar that nobody else remembered what I talked about.

At the care home one day the nurses told John that his wife was ill and they did not think she could live through it this time. He wept and pled with them to save her. "Do anything," he said. "I can't let her go."

"I prayed," he told me. "I prayed so hard. I told God I can't live without her. Please don't take her away."

She lived a little longer. He survived her death but not for long.

His daughter was bereft at the loss of her 100-year-old father.

Life is such a wonderful puzzle. I never get to the bottom of it.

When I went to visit Meg on the Monday before Thanksgiving, I was afraid it would be my last opportunity to see her. And I had expected to see her in bed but found her sitting in a recliner in her living room with a blanket across her lap.

She smiled and lifted her arms to hug me, put a kiss on my cheek, and declared immediately that she was getting better every day. I agreed, telling her that the Lord is building us up on the inside, even when we are wasting away on the outside. And she assured me that she and Howard believed in prayer.

While we were saying these things I moved a straight chair close so that I could touch her. Her white hair was clipped close to her head, like a crew cut, the same length all over her head. It was cute. She was paler than when I had seen her a couple of weeks earlier, but she still had that sparkle in her eye.

She asked me to look on the table behind me and get something. "That round thing," she said. It was a styrofoam ball covered with small shells. She wanted to show me that she had been making Christmas ornaments. That's Meg, I thought, always doing something artsy and pretty.

"Everybody is coming for Christmas," she said, and named people, her children, their mates, grandchildren. "Probably," she confided, "it will be our last Christmas." She stated this like just a fact, a reason why it was going to be a special Christmas.

She showed me her cane, smooth polished wood, a little crooked, decorated down its length with painted flowers. She boasted that she had graduated from her walker, and the cane was enough. "It keeps me balanced," she said." But there seemed to be more than that; she loved that cane. Then she said she wanted to go outside and down the path toward the parking lot, but Howard said she could do that only if he was with her and holding her arm.

One thing on my mind was to tell Meg what an inspiration she has been to me, but she beat me to it. Right away she began telling me that I had been a blessing to her. When she was diagnosed with cancer, she said, she remembered that I survived colon cancer in Lebanon in the middle of a war. She had been encouraged by that, she said.

I told her then that her calmness and optimism had been an inspiration to me and to our whole church. We all talked behind her back, I said, about how amazing she was. That was true. For seven years we had kept being astonished that she stayed so cheerful and confident.

"There is still another blessing I want from you," I told her, "This is Thanksgiving week, and I want to hear you tell me what you are thankful for."

Immediately she said, "Oh, I have so much. I have had a long, wonderful life. Eighty-four years, full of happy things. I have a wonderful family, so many good friends."

She started talking then about some of her very special friends, and she told me a rather long story about why she was so proud of her children. It crossed my mind that she didn't sound like someone whose cancer had gone to her brain.

She wanted to know about me, "What are you doing now?" she said.

I told her what we were studying in the Bible study group I was leading and then about something I was writing. And I said, "Meg, you have aged so gracefully.

What would you say to younger people about how to do that?"

She seemed stumped, wanted a little time to think about it. Then she took all of about ten seconds to ponder it and said, "Enjoy every day."

Of course, I thought. What else would Meg say? Enjoying life was what she always did.

I had brought my Bible so I could share with her something from the scripture. So, sitting just at her knees I read that tiny little psalm, number 131, telling her in advance that I love it because the author thinks of himself as a child sitting on his mother's lap. He is a calm and satisfied child, not worrying about the big things he doesn't understand. His mother is God, and he is sitting on God's lap, not wanting anything in particular, content just to sit there.

I had meant to say that that's how I want to be at the end, just sitting contentedly on God's lap, but Meg was all about living today, not about dying, so I didn't say it.

She thanked me for the psalm, said it was wonderful.

She wanted to get up and show me something and jumped out of her chair so nimbly I didn't notice how she did it, and then she used the cane, held my arm and walked me down the hall to their bedroom where she told me about several pictures on the wall. One showed her two daughters as teenagers sitting in the leafy branches of a tree. One was a wedding, but the two children in it were what she wanted me to see. I liked the snapshot of Meg and Howard walking on a beach, holding hands, the wind blowing their clothes.

She stumbled a bit, walking back to her chair but did it quickly, not worried about anything. Safely back she said, "Don't be surprised if I come wobbling down the aisle at church on Sunday. I want to come."

Before I left, I prayed, holding her hand, thanking God for Meg and entrusting her to God's care.

I had expected to say goodbye, but I didn't. How can you say goodbye to someone who is so alive?

I Will Welcome the Silence

Today at Miracle Ear I learned something really interesting.

My hearing aids have collected information that the office computer can read. There is a record of my use of the aids during the approximate year and a half that I have had them. The computer translated this information off the little chip that has been in my ear and turned it into a pie chart which shows that, since I got them, I have worn my hearing aids an average of ten hours per day.

"That is excellent. I can't ask more of anyone," Cindy, the examiner said. Then she told me that most people who claim not to like their hearing aids have actually not worn them enough to benefit. And Miracle Ear has the evidence. That's the kind of thing the hearing aid people notice.

But I get other meanings from her data. Some of the facts seem to be really important information about my life. For instance, the evidence was there on the chart that half the time in these seventeen months there was absolute silence, no sound coming to the hearing aids in my ears.

"You," Cindy told me, "have spent 49% or your time in complete silence."

Incredulous, I needed time to think. This, I realized, does not include the hours that I sleep, nor even the hours when I am working a crossword puzzle or reading in bed before sleeping. It is just the time in which I am wearing my hearing aids.

In the fourteen hours in which I am not wearing them, I could be in such a noisy place that I don't want my hearing aids or maybe I just went somewhere, forgetting to put them in my ears after I washed my hair. But let's be honest. Most of those fourteen hours are deliberately quiet hours, and in my twenty-four hour day they are followed by ten hours plugged for sound, nearly five of those also in silence.

This information astonishes me. I am surprised to realize what a quiet life I have. I love quiet, except when I don't.

I come home from church at noon on Sundays and the silence of the long afternoon ahead is like a weight on my heart. Once I sent my daughter a text admitting, "Being alone is worse on Sundays than other days." And she replied immediately, "Because it is a rest day. We don't rest well alone."

I can remember what it was like when we were two here, when sometimes Wayne interrupted my thoughts while I was writing, and about the third time he popped into my office I was annoyed. Silence was something I valued then. Once, long before that, we were seven. Through those years of raising children, how I longed sometimes for silence. An hour at a stretch to think my own thoughts was a beautiful thing.

Is that what I have now? The time I wished for when I had a companion? The time I needed when we were seven, and the days were full of questions, chatter, cries and just plain racket?

This is a disconcerting thought, to say the least, that the golden silence I wished for, I now have and call it loneliness. I need to ponder this.

I don't recognize the silence as something I wanted. I am afraid of it. Sometimes on the road three miles from home, I dread arriving, knowing that this silence will jump at me when I open the door. In my grief support group people admit they turn on the television just to disrupt the quiet.

And I who so needed silence lived to hate it. To consider it the stale breath of death. The absence of a familiar voice. The missing shuffle of feet in morning slippers.

Part of the struggle of learning to live the life I have now has been learning to accept this emptiness. And finding a way to admit that I am still the woman who needed quiet and time alone. And now I have it.

Accepting this as a blessing has required effort, the overcoming of reluctance to accept any blessing made possible by my loss. It is like accepting the honor of performing Jeremy's wedding when I knew it would have been Wayne's honor if he had lived. I do want quiet and privacy to think these thoughts, but I would happily push the delete button and forget the whole thing for an afternoon visit with the one I miss.

But Wayne let me live my life. He respected my need and gave me space to do what I do. This has not eliminated the problem, but it has at least helped me. If I have an advantage now, I know he is happy for me to take it.

As much as I miss him first thing in the morning, I have learned to enjoy that first hour of my day. I open the curtains onto the quiet forest. And I sit with my coffee. The rising sun is behind me, its light falling into this room through the clerestory windows that Wayne and our sons so cleverly planned. The view I am facing is full of light and shadows, slowly, gently, silently changing. Into the silence I say, "Thank you." The thought is not even tied to the beauty of the earth, the newness of the day, my cup of coffee, my rocking chair, the calm beginning of whatever is coming. It is just for all of them together, or none of them, just life.

The silence is deep, my hearing aids still in their case. And I am a fortunate woman, alone for now with God, whose voice needs no amplification.

Cindy at Miracle Ear had other things, such a trove of information. (I asked her if the police knew about this. She smiled and said, "I have no voice recording, can't prove who spoke to you, only that there was speech.")

The next largest slice in my computer screen pie was one in which there had been very little sound, like whispers. Cindy wondered if I talk to myself. I admitted that I do.

A slightly smaller slice of my life was in a noisy place, lots of sound, suggesting numerous voices. She said, "I can tell you get out and mix with people."

In a very small slice of my pie there was nothing but music. I thought I should do something about making that slice bigger.

Still I am astonished by the knowledge that I have such a quiet life.

The hearing aids seem to lie, because I do plenty to disturb the wonderful silence. I make noise, lots of noise that my hearing aids know nothing about. If someone could read the record in my brain, they would know: I argue with people who never know I am arguing; I rant about things and no one hears my rant; I raise serious questions while I am reading; I debate with myself about what to eat as well as sticky moral issues; occasionally I shout Hallelujah; I write and hear the words in my head; a song arrives unbidden and sings to me; a tree falls in my inner forest and the roaring crash breaks my heart.

All of this without any impact on the little chip in my hearing aid.

The whole truth is I have more silence than I realized and less than my hearing aids think.

Home from Miracle Ear with clean hearing aids and all this new information, I am impressed by how much I am responsible for those long periods of quiet or at least the chance for quiet, when all the noise is in my head. I have to acknowledge that the sounds in my world are more output than input. I generate them myself. It is I who disturbs the peace; I am the noisy child who sometimes doesn't give God a space to get a word in sideways.

In my Christian view, I must use what I am given even when it is not what I asked for. In my determination to live with purpose, what should I do with hours of solitude? What shall I choose to hear? What kinds of voices will I permit in my head? What will I create with this time? What will be my attitude toward this blessing rising out of loss?

I am trying to learn how to welcome the silence and be thankful.

I Will Play

Don't misunderstand. The resolve to play is serious for me.

The inability to play was something I did not like about my mother. Three of us girls were near the same age and so many games needed four people, but no matter how much we begged, she would not play. In fact she said critical things about people who had nothing better to do than play Old Maid.

Then I grew up to be a woman who worked her silly head off. Wayne used to chide me for not playing enough, and I always said that I would enjoy playing after I had my work done. I did learn, of course, that children learn by playing, and we teach them by playing with them. And I did notice how much we can learn about other people by playing games with them. How creative they can be, how honest, how able to laugh at their own mistakes.

And in the middle of Middle Eastern wars I learned how necessary it was when shells were falling to get invested in something that didn't matter. I manage sometimes to apply that to putting off cleaning up the kitchen.

Lunch out with the Red Hatters is one of the ways I play.

This is the old childhood game, a girl's-only club created for a certain limited group. If you are not getting old and proud of it, you are a misfit here. Sourpusses tend to drop out.

It is little girls dressing up in clothes not their own. I don't wear to Red Hat lunch the clothes of that woman who goes to church on Sunday morning, nor the clothes of that woman who cooks and cleans in blue jeans and writes in pjs and a robe.

I am gorgeous in my red and purple. Passing men tell me so. People in the street smile. Waiters know which group I am looking for. I meet other aged girls, all appropriately gorgeous. We compliment one another and admire one another's shoes and the bracelets on our arms. We talk about our hair and boast of the bargain we got on our blouse; we pass around pictures of beautiful grandchildren. If anybody has been to the E.R. we want to hear the details, here where troubles are all minor and transient. Anybody who has a birthday this month gets a hilarious card, chosen by our "Queen Mum," and it travels around the table, creating laughter as it goes. We share reactions to the menu, debating: the soup or the salad? the salmon or the steak? We eat something full of calories, with flavor that can only be imagined in our own kitchens. The waiter brings piles of take home boxes. And then we order ice cream.

For two hours the world is a party.

Occasionally, some kill-joy type of little devil whispers in my ear that the Red Hat Society is a waste of time and money. When this happens I stop to notice what has happened through years of sharing laughs and meals and shopping tips and sympathy and see that if I don't go I will not see my friends.

And on the way home we will stop at Trader Joe's and act like responsible grown-ups.

I love basketball. Everybody who knows me knows I am a basketball nut. It all started when I was thirteen years old, and in these seventy-five years basketball has only gotten better. I know there is much more pushing and hacking than there used to be. It was a finesse game once, and I liked that. But it is faster now, and kids start sooner so by the time they get to college their skill level is spectacular.

During basketball season I take a lot of mini-vacations in front of the television. I develop preferences for certain teams; I collect favorite players and even get attached to coaches whose styles I like. I am a fan of teams that whisk the ball around the court as though nobody knows or cares who gets to shoot. I like big rainbow shots that fall straight into the strings, and those quick little loopers that surprise the defense. The basic layup never gets old, but I don't much like the slam dunk. (If it is illegal for the defensive man to put his hand inside the rim, it should be illegal for his offensive opponent.) But, of course, the alley-oop really is a thing of beauty.

For the past twenty years March Madness has been my second favorite time of year, just after Christmas. Wayne and I always watched the tournament together. We clipped a bracket out of the newspaper and filled it in to predict the outcome, and at the end of every game we recorded the results.

This year, my first March Madness without him, I thought I should fill in a bracket, though it would be harder alone. In the process I texted my grandson Sam to ask his opinion about who would be the champion. He told me which team he was choosing, a dark horse with a lot of talent, not the one I thought. Then he invited me to join the group he had formed on ESPN, explaining that it was just a little friendly competition between friends, no money involved.

I thought, Why not? That sounds like a lot more fun than rooting all alone. So I got on ESPN, filled-in all the blanks and there I was in a group of young twenties people, who didn't have a clue who I was.

Well, if you are a fan, you know that 2018 was the most unpredicted tournament in history. Upsets began in the first round, busting my bracket on day one, and surprises just kept happening. None of us in our group made outstanding scores, but when the tournament came down to Michigan or Villanova, there were just two of us with a chance. Michigan would make Sean the winner in our group, and Sean's opinion certainly had merit. On that last night Michigan played valiantly. But Villanova lived up to my expectations. So there I was at the end: on the top of the heap, though with nothing much to brag about.

I have to say that was fun, a good way to play basketball when you are eighty-eight. Anonymously. Incognito. Sam was the only one of those twenty-something people who knew it was his grandma who beat them all.

So many times I have been invited. So many times I had a conflict or a different need, so I apologized. I admit that the name did not excite me. Hand and Foot? A card game?

It reminded me of our friend Paul Smith, playing Rook on the beach at Aqaba in his bathing suit, sitting on the sand, leaning against the back of an upside down folding chair, with his cards between his toes.

Finally, I went. What a revelation! A game that needs six decks. Six decks need a mechanized shuffler; otherwise we will be here all day. Or maybe, as another friend of mine insists, "This is not a game, just an excuse to spend an afternoon chattering about nothing."

"A simple game of luck," the experienced players tell me at the beginning. And every time I put down a card a new illogical rule surfaces. We have partners. (I am still not sure that the way we share information is ordinarily permitted.) We collect things: everybody wants the same thing. Except certain cards that are red hot; I need to get rid of them as soon as possible. Stacks line up around the table. We put certain cards on top to identify each pile. Black and red don't always refer to colors. I see the game as a creative way to reshuffle six decks, collecting categories, and getting it done first. The scorekeeper needs a calculator. I am spectacularly successful, my brilliance irrelevant. Everyone knows about beginner's luck.

For two hours I forget to worry about war in the Middle East and whether or not the president will be impeached. I almost forget that my back is hurting.

My son Tim says putting the pressure somewhere else is a vacation. I pressured my brain to remember 100 rules, and the principle: do everything in order.

The experiment was so successful I came home and fell asleep.

I Will Throw Away My Own Trash

I intend to clean up my space, as I leave it.

This seems to be the courteous thing to do, like picking up the trash you drop on a hiking trail. It is good for the environment and a favor to the stranger-brother who is walking behind you.

But what I intend is not easy. I need to live in the house and at the same time pack it up to leave, because, you see, I don't know when I am leaving.

I have so many questions:

Between now and then will I need two umbrellas?

Must I keep tax records for three years or is it seven?

Will anyone want an eel skin brief case?

Will my grandchildren wonder what happened to those dear little art objects they made for me, if they are not here when I am gone?

How many pairs of slipper socks can one woman use?

Do I have time to look at all these pictures once more?

Will I read this book finally if I take it to the assisted-care home (the assisted-care home I am hoping never to go to)?

And how can I possibly consign to a burn pile these photos of my high school friends? Much less, this file of letters from my dead husband.

You see, it is not simple.

Still, doing it is thoughtful and fair. I want my children to be able to get on with their lives unencumbered.

And there are other things, surprising benefits to getting rid of things.

I am reminded of something a Lebanese man told me early in his country's civil war. Bombs had destroyed the house he inherited from his parents, along with most of his personal possessions. He told me that he was briefly bereft, then overcome with an exhilarating freedom. He could now decide where to go. And he could go without any baggage.

When Wayne and I moved into this house, we expressed to one another the hope that we would never again have to move what we called "this stuff."

"Next time we go," we promised one another, "it will be to the place where we can take nothing with us."

The hated part of traveling is packing and unpacking. We thought we would not have to do this anymore.

But my house, like many other houses, has managed to hoard literally hundreds of items that will be considered trash when I am gone. Already a hoard of them is not useful to the current inhabitant.

Wayne had a way of seeing the practical value in objects that appeared to me to be useless. His shop has shelves loaded with small items for which I don't even have names. He delighted in saying to me, "See this little thing (a nut, a bolt, a board, a nameless little strip of metal). I have had it for forty years and today I need it." The strange part is that he even knew where to find it.

Once in the middle of the night I overturned the insulated cup on my bedside table. It landed upside down on its straw which I discovered in the daylight now had a one inch length-wise slit. When I tried to drink I got nothing but air.

When night came again, the straw had been fixed, the slit sealed with a little plastic tube through which the straw fit perfectly. I asked Wayne where he got that little plastic tube, and he said, "I found it in the front yard."

When, after Wayne's death, I told our son Jim about this, he said, "Did you ask him how many years ago he found it?"

I had not thought to ask that. It was a good question. But the imminent question now is: what to do with all this wealth of small objects that only Wayne knew the value of? For sure he went empty-handed, but he left me with a lot of strange thing-a-majigs and doodads with potential value to a frugal and inventive man.

I sometimes ask a helpful neighbor, "What is this good for?"

I take pictures with my phone, relay them to one of my sons and ask, "Do you know why your dad saved this?"

If no one knows what to do with it, this must be permission to throw it away.

This week I called our county Waste Management office to ask for instructions on how to get rid of certain dead items that are cluttering my space. And I feel freer already imagining this old and crippled grill picked up at the curb and these plastic buckets dumped out of my recycling bin into that noisy truck and carried away.

When my carport is spacious and clean, I think I will wash the car.

While Wayne collected useful paraphernalia, I tended to collect pretty things: candle sticks, vases just the right color for my dining room, original paintings by starving artists, delicate embroidered napkins and runners. And people give me things: teacups and platters, notecards and pens, and scarves, especially scarves and shawls, lovely things, soft and warm, long and elegant, shimmering, in every color I might want.

Giving things away is, I think, a good way to go. It is like recycling, giving objects a new reason to exist. It is fun. It makes me feel generous, even if I actually just want to be rid of the stuff. And when I give away objects I treasure, this makes me feel I am protecting things by finding them another home.

I have a growing list:

1. All sweaters I have not worn for three years. Sweaters take a lot of space in my closet. I am running out of space. Somebody with space in her closet and cold arms needs a sweater.

2. Sleeping bags I don't need unless I go camping. Their absence will provide a much needed excuse not to go camping. I just don't want ever again to wake in the middle of the night, warm in my sleeping bag, in a cold tent forty yards from the bathroom. And I pray to be spared from being a refugee.

3. Several pairs of shoes that hurt my feet. With the wisdom of the old, I have weighed beauty against comfort and made my decision. I will wear enough beautiful jewelry that no one will notice my feet.

4. The pretty candle-holder that I forgot I had, along with my regret for not using it during the holidays. If I put it back in the cupboard I might again forget it is there, and finding it again will prove I am silly. I hate knowing I am silly.

5. Books: Titles I read once, and once was enough. And books I would like to read again but don't have time for because of all the new books that young geniuses keep spewing out and the library buys with the money they make from selling my Shakespeare and Thomas Wolfe and fifth grade geography.

Last Christmas I made a game of giving away some of my miniature vases. Through the years I managed to collect a whole shelfful of these tiny ornaments: blown glass from Lebanon, olive wood from Palestine, pottery from Cyprus and Tennessee, alabaster from Egypt, and even some hand-painted wooden pieces from Russia. I wrapped them, one for every member of our big family, and put numbers on the packages. Then everyone drew numbers and, in order, each person chose a package and opened it. Number two could "steal" the gift that number one had opened or choose another, and so on. You know the game—any single vase could be stolen no more than three times.

There were many surprises, a little envy, and in the end some friendly trading. In the process everyone present at the party got a souvenir of Grandma's roaming the world, while Grandma herself decreased the clutter in her china cabinet.

Making a will is important. I don't mean a legal document, just a personal plan, written down, for taking care of things I value.

For instance, I have this glass bowl beautifully painted by my friend Ramona who had a progressive disease that was taking away all of her ability to move. Just able to wiggle her right wrist up and down, she put the precise geometric pattern on this bowl. So much do I love Ramona and her bowl that I can't bear to think of leaving the earth without giving it a safe place to be.

In Lebanon once, feeling its fragility in a very dangerous world, I hid this bowl in a cavity within the stone wall of the house. Surrounded by stone and invisible, it did not know that the earth shook and shrapnel fell on the roof.

Who will get it when I go? That's a secret.

And, O.K. I have to give up some things—some lovely, useless objects, but mostly file drawers full of paper, random collections of words—that are precious to me but meaningless to everyone else in the world. What makes this hard is that it requires an admission that pieces of my life cannot be felt or appreciated by anyone else. They die with me.

There are traps in this process. Part of the experience is rational, part purely emotional. It is the emotional part of the process that makes it so time-consuming and exhausting. Some ridiculously irrational choices will be made.

This week I went through a file of old greeting cards. Obviously, I lacked the courage to throw them away without looking at them one more time. After all, they were kept because they touched me when I received them, because the source was impressive or because the message was one I wanted to read again. But they have been in this drawer, some for two years, some for fifteen, without being looked at again. I asked myself if anyone else wants to see them, decided not and began tossing.

A few, however, I had to keep. A particular letter because it is the last I ever received from my friend. Another because the sender has disappeared out of my life, and I need to use this address to see if it still works. Normally the envelopes are gone already; we wrote the addresses on the cards and then discarded the envelopes, but several cards from my husband were still in the original envelope. I removed them and put the whole batch of them in a binder. I will mark it for destruction when I am gone.

Nearly done with this chore, I was left with an empty red envelope with one word written on it in Wayne's unique handwriting. The word was the silly, sweet nickname he used to address me in warm moments. I considered keeping it. How? For what? Then I tossed it into the waste basket and left the room. A few minutes later I came back with a trash bag to put into it this heap of paper that had to be discarded. For a few moments I stared at the red envelope in the top of waste basket. Then I took it out and put in on my desk.

Today I was so bold as to open the file of my mother's letters, her short weekly updates about who was coming to visit, which flower was blooming in her yard, what she was making for lunch, along with reports on my daddy's long-dying with emphysema and the treatments for her arthritis. Usually on blue air letter forms, these messages were brief, poorly punctuated and creatively spelled, but they communicated love and concern, along with the repetitious details of daily life in a small town in Louisiana. Individually they tended to sound insignificant, but collectively they were essential like bread. For many years while I lived in places far and strange to her, nothing but these letters held us together.

So why are they now trash? Because I have not looked at them for twenty years, because no one else in the world would truly understand them, and I am preparing my house for another generation, or strangers.

When I vowed to do this, to throw away my own trash, I knew it would be emotional. Now it feels like throwing away my mother. What she was like is in the letters. What she would say. The way she would say it. The proof that she lived. How will the world know?

I keep figuring out ways to compromise. I could just keep a couple of these birthday cards as samples of her handwriting, especially the unique way she wrote the capital F of Frances. (It took my second grade teacher about a year to persuade my fingers to write it in another way.)

Our trash is full of little treasures and traps.

If you pay attention you can learn a lot from your trash. In one day, reading old letters from just one year I learned all of this:

The dead keep speaking to you, if you reread their letters.

I am capable of relearning things I knew long ago and forgot.

We were invited to a lot of places we never went.

I can feel sorry all over again that my kid was looking for a job and didn't have money to pay the rent while I was on the other side of the world.

Something I was stressed and distressed about in 1991 has devolved into a useless mystery.

My grandchildren said such cute things when they were little.

Love twenty-seven years old is still good news.

A compliment only gets better with age.

Some questions have been on my mind for many years and remain without answers.

Undated letters describing transformative events are like limbs severed from the body of history.

The handwriting of the beloved deceased is valuable like an old, old work of art.

Today I threw away:

A barely legible note from a dear friend, dead ten years now, who was going blind. The lines were fairly straight; she was using a guide of some kind. Already I wish I had it back, because I did not memorize what it said.

An original poem, long and humorous, that functioned as an invitation to a unique wedding that was not enough to stick those two people together for good. It was a well-crafted, clever piece of work, that poem. It deserved a better fate than the city dump.

A crudely printed boastful note from an innocent child who has disappeared now inside a savvy young business consultant.

A letter from a friend explaining why she does not believe in "a god" anymore, along with her mission statement for fighting cancer. She survived a long time.

And that file, the whole thing, my mother's letters.

As I threw these things away I made a record, because letting them go was such hard work.

Lately I got to wondering about the trash in my head: unanswerable questions with power to keep me awake; salacious rumors; false impressions of my neighbor; trivia for which I have no filing cabinet.

A sleep expert says this is one thing that happens in our brains when we sleep. The brain throws out the useless things that it had to absorb in the day but now deems unimportant. This causes me to explore the links between what I consciously keep in my brain and what I have lost or keep losing. Some things made an indelible impression, while I was not conscious of it, while I had no way of knowing it was important. And then there are memories I have kept deliberately, long after I should have let them go. I conclude that my brain, while I am asleep and unable to interfere, tries to protect itself from useless stuff. Awake, I do not cooperate well with this effort.

This is why throwing away trash is so difficult. All these physical things, these objects, this paper, are metaphors for some inner reality. Endowed with a kind of electricity, they stick to my fingers. I shake them over the wastebasket, they cling to my flesh.

I Will Choose My Battles

It was the weekend before Thanksgiving. I had guests coming, pie crust to make, vegetables to buy, a slightly scratchy throat, a friend dying, a basketball game I wanted to see, a granddaughter requesting prayer for a painful problem, and a 416-page book to read in a few days. An hour away an entire town was on fire, so like everybody else in the area I had a small suitcase packed, my emergency bag ready to grab in case I needed to flee.

All of this I accepted as part of a normal life until I opened my computer and discovered 73 unread emails in my box. It was the emails that got my attention. I started to wonder: Is it appropriate for an 89-year-old woman to have so much to think about?

Eighty percent of friends my age have died; I have no employer. My children call; my grandchildren text. But somehow I have inherited the world. People with dreams tell me about them. Organizations with worthy causes need my help. Politicians share their outrage. In a state 2000 miles away an election will be lost, unless I send three dollars. Writers I really like have posted new blogs and I have not yet read the previous one. Every company I ever bought anything from wants to sell me something else. Out of the population of 300,000,000 I have been chosen to fill out a survey, and the fate of civilization hangs on my opinion.

Some of these messages were leftovers from previous days, because I failed to keep up. So, by creating a new folder and moving emails, I reduced the number 73 to 55, in the process changing nothing.

I had to admit that my eclectic interests had begun to produce an overload in every part of my life: my email box, my budget, my prayers, my schedule. I can't be informed about it all, pay for it all, appeal to God about it all, much less work for it all.

Something has to go. How do I make that happen? How do I choose my own battles?

I decided to make a list of some criteria that should help me decide which pressing issues rate a place in my life. Perhaps:

1. The matter's ultimate importance to the world (narrowed down to its importance to me)

2. The urgency of the situation (my time is short)

3. My certainty that I am on the right side of the issue (I am convinced enough to take a public stand)

4. The way it relates to my own knowledge, values and faith (a natural choice)

5. The extent to which life has prepared me to face it (I have relevant experience)

6. My actual existing opportunity to make a difference (at least a hint of realism involved)

7. Time and energy that I can commit to it.

Let me consider this list a tool and try it. Suppose someone wants to lead me into growing vegetables for the poor in cities. This is important to the world and to me. I care. Hunger is an urgent matter. Enough calories and proper nutrition are undeniably good. But the way this matter relates to my talent is a bust. Life has not prepared me to do it, my thumbs are every color but green, and the ground in my backyard is hopelessly rocky. I say no to this challenge. Please take this request somewhere else.

How about taking a stand for peace in the world, advocating for a U.S. Department of Peace? The importance of this issue to the world and to me is major, even critical, I am convinced, to our survival. It is urgent because of the destructive power that exists and the animosities. I know I am on the right side, even convinced that the Creator of the world is on this same side. This need relates to considerable knowledge, gained by experience, backed up by study, and it fits like a banana in its peeling with my personal values and faith.

I see war as the collection of all the evils in this world. Life has prepared me to illustrate this with war stories personally experienced or observed. Furthermore, even my limited experience in administration clarifies the principal that nothing gets done until it is on someone's job description. The presence or absence of a Department of Peace expresses louder than any policy statement the philosophy and focus of a nation. And I do not speak alone. Numerous organizations and politicians are also dedicated to this cause, opening for me doors of opportunity. Clearly this is for me.

See, the tool seems to work. I can choose this struggle and make it my own, though there is still that last factor: personal time and energy.

My silence on many worthy causes will mean, not that I have no interest but simply that I am unable to fight on numerous fronts. A lifelong fault has caught up with me in old age. Having too many concerns, I am now making difficult choices.

Writing this, I may give the impression that I am in control or think I am. I am not, of course. But I am making progress.

As time goes by I will choose fewer and fewer battles. Already I delete, unread, eighty percent of my emails, doing it with minimal guilt. Some battles are no longer mine. I have willed them to a younger generation.

May God give them courage, and wisdom.

I Will Text

Last night I suffered a small disaster. At least I thought so.

Preparing to travel, needing to make sure my daughter-in-law remembered that she was taking me to the airport, I sent her a text. Right away my phone told me: Failed! I sent it again. Failed!

I sent one to my son, the man likely to be by her side at that hour. Failed! I tried their daughter. Failed!

Right away I started thinking that I did something wrong. Because in the morning I had tried to establish a new account for a different service, and I came to the point where the system asked for a phone number to which they could send a text, and I gave this number and then I never got a text.

Now it occurs to me that I might have thought that was the point at which my texting failed, but instead I thought, silly me, I have screwed things up.

Disaster! Traveling all day, I can't notify my half of the world where I am at every moment.

I resorted to calling. I talked on the phone with my smart twenty-something granddaughter who sympathetically but calmly told me that had happened to her. She turned off her phone and turned it on again and her texting came back magically.

I turned off my phone and turned it on again, and nothing changed. I had to go to bed with this life-crippling problem unsolved.

This morning, while drinking my wake-up coffee, I decided to prove one more time that my texting was dead. And right away the system told me: Delivered.

Sometimes thinking there is a disaster is the disaster.

But this is not why I am telling this story. My hope is to impress somebody, any one of the half dozen people left in the world who do not text, that the inability to do so is a major loss.

In fact I can name several whom I respect deeply, smart people, purposeful people who have decided not to text. They do email and actually open their letters, some not every day, and they seem to be totally modern people, but they refuse to communicate by way of cryptic notes, ignoring spelling and rules of grammar. That's O.K. I can keep on respecting them though I don't share their point of view.

I bothered to tell one of them why I decided to text. "To communicate with my grandchildren."

He replied, "If my grandchildren want to communicate with me they can call me on the phone."

And I said, "Good luck with that."

I understand why young people don't phone while running from history class to chemistry lab, from lab to swim practice, swim practice to the dining hall, dining hall to In-'N-Out for work. I even know they can't receive calls in the offices and ICU wards and coffee bar windows where they work.

I wouldn't phone either to tell kids in L.A., "It's snowing here." But if I text them, I can expect an answer: "Oh, I'm so jealous," they say. And both of us will remember the happy times they had here as little kids tobogganing down the hill behind our house on Christmas holidays.

I don't phone a boy in Virginia to say, "Did you have a good game today?" But a text will get a text back, "Won big time. Went two for three, got an RBI and two steals." A young man will remember his grandma is his fan, and she will know the significant stats. He is still good, in an adult league.

One of my granddaughters, shortly after getting her first phone, said this famous thing on the way to church one Sunday. "I am trying so hard to be a hip teenager, but I am a failure. It is 10:00 A.M. already; I have had only one text today and that was from my mother."

Having heard about this incident, I knew exactly what to do at the end of a day when I was trying to learn to text. Realizing that I had received not one text from anyone that day, I wrote one to 'Nessa and told her, "As a hip grandma, I am a failure."

She wrote back immediately, "Oh, Grandma, I know exactly how you feel. I am happy to help you out."

See what I mean? It is fun. It communicates. It works across age gaps. We are in touch. That is the important thing. Those little touches are like dabs of glue holding us together between visits.

Texting is really useful.

During the civil war in Lebanon, Wayne and I, along with most of the population, learned not go anywhere without telling someone where we were going and the route we intended to take. By the time we moved to the foothills of the Sierras, reporting our location was an ingrained habit. After we learned to text, Wayne began to use his phone, without calling, to report to me and sometimes half the family about his whereabouts. If he went to Placerville, half an hour from home, he would send me texts constantly. "Done at doctor, pharmacy now. Need anything?" On a trip to Southern California, when it was my turn to drive, he would sit in the passenger seat sending texts, reporting our location to those we had left in the morning and those who were expecting us for dinner. And when I was away he would send me texts like this: "If driving send me a blank, so I will know you are O.K."

Making phone calls was difficult. Texting was a lifeline for this gregarious, loving and nearly deaf man. It was a blessing.

And one more thing. Sometimes people have to put their phones in a silent mode. They are in a meeting or taking a test, and it mustn't ring, but an urgent written message will still get through. I was in a meeting when I got the message that Sam's baseball team had won the Virginia state championship.

Picture this: I did something foolish and broke my back. In a standing position, I snapped a vertebra. I heard it, felt it, knew it. I was alone in a strange community, upstairs in a house where no one was expected for two hours.

Because I had learned to text on my tablet, which happened to be reachable, I was able to communicate with Jan who was in a meeting and she got to me while I was still using my arms to support my weight, keeping the pressure off a broken back. I not only text, I have reasons to be grateful for it.

But texting is just a metaphor here for what I really want to say. New things come along in the world, demanding new skills. Young people seem to intuit what to do with these, but we elderly people need lessons and demonstrations, and sometimes we don't learn on the first try, because truthfully we come to them unprepared and a little afraid.

I was fifty-five when I got my first computer. Long before that I knew that the computer was a necessary invention and a boon to our publishing house. The first one we bought was for Wayne, because he was our bookkeeper. Then I bought them for all our editors. I watched all those people learn, providing tutors and manuals. Then finally I got one myself and sat down in front of it with awe.

We happened to be in the U.S., so it was our son Tim who gave me my first lessons. He began by saying, "Mom, you are smart. This thing is just a dumb machine. It can't do anything except what you tell it to do."

Thank you, Tim.

I admit that brains start to slow up. I can't tell you why, but things do get harder. However, that is only part of the problem. When we are almost ninety new technology is baffling because it was not part of our education. (It is entirely possible that when today's teen-agers are eighty, they will have the same problem we have now with something the world has not heard of yet.)

But we are still smarter than the machine. It has to obey us. We just have to learn the commands, and we can do it. Not with the speed of an ice skater, but if we need to do something we can still learn how. Not with the grace of an ice skater either. We won't glide; we will stumble. Doesn't matter. And it is not our fault; the technology just arrived a little late.

Just while writing this book I learned (by searching online) that there is a program for teaching elderly people how to use all this modern technological equipment. Susan Nash, who directs this school for seniors, has been named by Stanford University as one of the fifty outstanding influencers in the many aspects of aging.

And I will learn to use the newest Windows, because I have to. It came in my new computer. If I am going to write, I need it. And here I am, writing.

There is a common idea that elderly people who have lost some of their faculties are in a second childhood. I remember being provoked myself when I was about forty by an old man, because he was helpless and not willing to make his own sandwich. I said (to myself) that he acted like a two-year-old. What was I thinking? This was an insult to two-year-olds. A two-year-old would say, "Let me!" He would make a mess of it, but he would eat his mess and be happy. The truth is that a two-year-old is in a very fast learning stage, so much so that there is a vast difference between a barely-two-year-old, and one who is almost three.

A two-year-old who is almost three will never give up. My grandson Sam when he was nearly three and about as tall as a duck aspired to shoot a standard basketball into a standard hoop, ten-feet off the ground. I knew he couldn't and got very tired of waiting and chasing the ball and telling him, "Come on. We need to go now."

He wouldn't quit. It was as though having the ball in his hands again made him forget the failures. He stopped only when he had done it! I promise you he did it. That's what children do.

These days a lot of elderly people are having a second youth. Just a couple of weeks ago I got an email from a friend of mine asking me how to go about setting up a website. He has some interesting material he has written in recent years and is thinking of publishing it a piece at a time as blogs. Though my advice is not that of an expert, I told him what I knew from experience and thought nothing more about it until right now when I realize what happened. This ninety-year-old asked me, an eighty-eight year-old, how to set up a website. Is that surprising? Funny? Or outrageously cool? Actually, that's just the way the world is happening now. The psychological age of my wonderful friend is nearly three, trying to be fifteen.

I too can do new things and be elated that I did them.

A few weeks ago I learned something new. I taught myself to use the power washer.

You don't want to know the whole story of my clumsiness, and the mistakes I made. But I learned five things:

1. Dragging a heavy vacuum-in-reverse with electric wires and two hoses, one of them two hundred feet long and full of water, over rocks, around corners and up steps is a challenge to an old lady's muscular fitness.

2. Water under force will peel the paint off your house.

3. No amount of water under force will make a spider web turn loose from a window.

4. Somebody will surely think soon of an easy high-tech way to wash the mold off my patio.

5. The water company will charge you thirty dollars extra to get this knowledge by experience.

Still trying to discover where my grandchildren are, I have been forced to get an Instagram account. That is working out a little better than power washing the house.

Snow

I live on top of a hill, and I don't have four-wheel drive. When it snows those lucky people who do can go down to church or to work or a store or a medical appointment with confidence that they can get back home again. I cannot.

Fifteen years ago this was not a problem. We went down whenever we wanted; dressed for church, we would throw our boots into the back seat and go. If, when coming back, we spun our wheels on the steep hill, we would coast to the bottom and park that useless car. We would then put on our boots and hike, zigzagging up the road to reduce the effect of gravity, feeling exhilarated on arrival.

No more can I even consider such a challenge, but neither am I complaining.

I love snow for the simple beauty of it. I know it can be a terrible inconvenience. I know it can be dangerous. I know it can be tiresome to people who live in Minnesota. My husband was one of those; he had stories about snow piled on snow all winter until it was up to the eaves of his house. He was the kid who had to shovel, repeatedly all winter, a path from the door to the woodshed.

When we first moved to these foothills, I would wake early just because there was snow, the way a kid wakes before dawn on Christmas morning. As soon as I had a cup of coffee I would get into my warmest clothes and my only boots and go for a walk before anyone or anything had spoiled the pristine perfection of the world. I took my little camera and snapped everything as I walked—panoramas of the empty street, houses dressed for a holiday, towering frosted pines. I took close-ups of bending branches, cottony balls clinging to tree bark, a turban-shaped hat on a red fire hydrant, and on the way back the empty white holes my feet made, as I stepped in each again in hope of disturbing a perfect world as little as possible.

When I got back home my energetic husband would have the fire blazing and pull off my boots and smile at my descriptions.

I would send film off in the mail and get back pictures, sending the best to my mother in Louisiana.

Now, in the most recent winter of my eighties, I enjoy the snow by staying home. I open the curtains, sacrificing some warmth, since these curtains are lined especially to protect me from the cold glass, and I sit in front of the fire to stare out at the tangles of frosted branches in the forest, guess the depth of the white topping on the deck railing, marvel at the way snow defies gravity by clinging to the uprights like lace on a lady's bodice. Sometimes I venture, in pajamas and robe, so far as the front stoop to photograph the expanse of pure white between my door and the trees and once again I try but fail to capture the gleaming splendor of sun on snow.

I have a pot of creamy soup made. Debating the possibility of putting on real clothes, I notice the little lights all over the tree limbs, bright drops of melting winter, glistening in the sun. I worship while the snow slides off the skylights.

Whatever I enjoyed before, when I was young and strong and adventurous, I can still enjoy. I will find a way. Some by watching instead of performing. Some by listening instead of speaking. Some by sending instead of going. Some by praying instead of doing. Some by remembering and being thankful. The best pictures I ever took are stored in my head.

If I review what I have loved in this world, as I sometimes do in my old age, I have to put snow high on the list. And right after snow, hot soup in the kitchen and a warm rice bag at my feet in the bed.

I Will Be Responsible for Security

People worry about me. Sometimes that feels like a nuisance. I am an adult. I get in the car and go places. And since there is nobody in this house but me, I can't say, "Honey, I'm running to the store for some milk. Anything I can do for you while I'm out?"

There is nobody to respond by sending me to the hardware store for some screws "just like this one, same size." Nobody to know how long I am gone. That is a sad fact, but it leaves me free. And irresponsible. If I notice a flowering tree by the road just beyond the store and feel like a little drive to welcome spring, I can just go. Right?

Right. Almost.

There are people whose imaginations get away from them if they call twice in half an hour and I don't pick up the phone. I am trying to learn to like that.

Once I was in my own house. It was summer, very hot, an ideal time to do that chore in the library, because my library is in my basement that is so cool. I meant to be half an hour, but some book just sucked me in, and I forgot passing time. I even forgot that I had no house phone down there and had left my cell upstairs in my purse.

Kim, this nice, respectful fellow church member, just wanted to know if I could come to a committee meeting on Thursday afternoon at 4:00. When I didn't answer my phone she moved me to the bottom of her list to call later, like fifteen minutes later. And she did this for several hours, becoming more and more concerned. It happens, you see, that Kim had a scary memory about a neighbor who lived alone; the gentleman owned the property next door to hers, but they couldn't actually see one another from their homes. An elderly man, he fell in his backyard and couldn't get up. It was three days before anyone missed him enough to go to his house and find him. He survived, but barely.

So Kim showed up, pounding on my door. It was night already. She said, "I can't go to bed, because you won't answer your phone."

I was sorry and surprised and grateful and starting to catch on. People feel responsible for one another. That is a wonderful thing.

At the same time I'm thinking: I may be almost ninety, but I am well, I have my wits, and I can take care of myself. I know, my family knows, my friends and neighbors know. But, at the same time, they realize, and I agree, that what I can do doesn't cover the unexpected moment when I can't. My own competence is enough, until I fall down the stairs. It works, until I withdraw to the basement and have a heart attack.

And the fact that I am well right now doesn't seem to comfort other people, the people who want to get here fast if I am in trouble. This is a conundrum. While I feel perfectly safe, I have to think about other people.

What is my responsibility to the people who care about me?

A friend of mine in a distant city told me about a great system that a certain big church used to take care of its elderly people. They had a call system that worked like this: Group A, a long list of elderly or handicapped people all knew they would get a phone call every morning by a given hour; Group B, a list of volunteers each had one person to call. If the call did not get an answer, the first step of an emergency plan went into effect.

One evening one of those elderly women in Group A fell in her bathroom. She was not badly hurt, but she could not get up. She lay there on the bath mat and thought, "I will be fine here until 8:30 in the morning. The phone will ring, and when I don't answer, someone will come."

For several days I thought about this. I thought that I might initiate such a program in my small rural church, but honestly, it was a little hard for me to say that somebody needs to call me every morning at the same time to make sure I am alive and standing on my feet.

Then I thought, Why do I have to put this on somebody else? Why can't I call some designated person every morning to report the good news?

I chose my daughter-in-law who lives half an hour away. Sylvia is smart and nervy. She would call the fire department to report that she saw the fire chief smoking.

I chose to text. I told her what I meant to do. No text would imply something was wrong. I couldn't get out of bed. I was kidnapped during the night. I fainted in the kitchen. I am getting too old and forgetful to do what I promise to do.

So, we agreed. Every morning now, soon after I get up, I send Sylvia a text and tell her what I am doing. She answers with hearts and smiley faces. Except when I forget. When I forget, she sends me a text, ending with a question mark.

If I don't answer the text, my phone rings.

It is true that I can't be totally responsible for my own security. What I can be responsible for is assuring others when I am well. This is half the reason for any security system.

Only after I proved that I could take first responsibility for myself did I mention the issue in a group of church friends. That caused Mary Ellen to turn me into her project. From one morning to the next is a long time, she thought. So she calls me every evening between 7:00 and 8:00. Not once has she forgotten me.

Meanwhile half the people I know have said I should get some kind of call button. And my sister, who is nearly ten years younger than I, broke her leg in her back yard in Albuquerque and spent four painful hours crying out for help before anyone heard.

I mentioned to my family that I preferred a solution that would not involve a monthly payment, and one of my brilliant sons came up with an idea. You know those gadgets that sit quietly on the coffee table until you call them by name and ask them to play Beethoven's Fifth Symphony? They would just as soon call Dwight or 911, or even order a pizza if I am hungry there on the bathroom floor. All I have to do is ask.

Now that I have all this in order and functioning, I'm scared to misbehave knowing I will get caught.

I Will Just Do It

Surprised once at something my mother had done in a very hard circumstance, I asked her how she had managed. She stared at me a moment as though she might not understand the question, sitting there with scrawny elbows on the arms of her rocker, a robe over her swollen, arthritic knees. She said, "Frances, when I have something to do, I just do it."

The words rang true, though I was really young then, maybe sixty-six. In my old age they seem to get more and more relevant to everything.

Rob, a fellow church member, and I were sitting across the table from one another at a Lenten supper. I happened to be upset about something and Rob is a good listener, so I spilled it.

Our grandson in the Special Forces somewhere in the Middle East had reported to his parents that his team had no food except Army rations which had proven to be neither the right food nor enough for them. Zach himself was hungry and had lost fifteen pounds in the first month of his deployment. I was more than puzzled that the Army could let this happen. I was outraged. The least any army could do for its soldiers was to feed them!

I suggested to Rob that when military action is required they might not be able to function well if they are hungry.

Rob told me that he had seen something about this on television. People were complaining that our soldiers were not being properly fed. That this might be happening to other units too was bad news to me.

Rob had to get up at that moment and play the role of Satan tempting Jesus in that evening's skit, so I stewed while he suavely told a very cool young Jesus why listening to him instead of God was the sensible thing to do.

When Rob came back to the table, he said, "It can't be about money. The military has lots of money; it can't be a lack of information; it has to be about logistics."

And I said, "But it certainly does not inspire confidence. What if, because of logistics, they don't have enough bullets or the radio dies and they don't have another one?"

"Besides," I said, "When military action is required, men who are hungry might not even think straight."

Then Rob, his face expressing a bit of doubt, told me about a soldier, who was cut off from the food supply with an important assignment. He was suffering from hunger and malnutrition, but he was able to do what he had been trained to do. He could not do other things, but, like a robot, he could do that one thing. I remembered then that those men in the Special Forces had endured extreme hunger during part of their training. They had been required to evade and escape a pursuing enemy while starving.

I went home and kept thinking about this. While thinking, I made Zach a double batch of those no-bake chocolate oatmeal cookies that he loves so much and mailed them to his APO address.

(I am still looking for a way to give the Army a piece of my mind.)

Later, at home, I remembered something out of my own experience.

The entire Near East Baptist Mission, twenty-four of us, were in Cyprus, having been ousted from Lebanon by the State Department. This was 1987; several Americans had been kidnapped in Lebanon. Unable to find or free them, our government had been embarrassed, and in reaction had ordered us to leave. The automatic penalty for our disobedience would be three years in prison.

It is impossible to explain in a paragraph what we had lost. Wayne and I had lived in Lebanon seventeen years; some had been there twenty-seven. In leaving, we had deserted duties and goals, homes, friends, promises, and some of us, even our possessions.

Stupid from sleeplessness and shock, we had been met by journalists and a couple of superiors responsible for figuring out what to do with twenty-four adults expelled from their assigned country. Where to send us now for some new task?

They gave us a day to rage and weep and a night to sleep before they began asking us questions about what we wanted to do now. They might as well have asked mannequins which dresses they wanted to wear.

Finally, one of the blank faces managed to express a preposterous wish. "Wherever you need us. We are ready to go anywhere, just so we can all go together."

The questioner, a sensitive, caring gentleman, trying hard not to call this idea insane, replied that he could not imagine how to do this. And another man in our group began to weep then, loudly, like a child.

On the third day a group of us were riding in a car on the way to a meeting where we had to deliver something close to a decision, a consensual leap from yesterday's tragedy to tomorrow's duty. We tried to talk about it; no one in the car was able to say anything substantive and intelligent, though behind the efforts were worthy intentions, courageous ideas. At some point I began to understand that somehow I had to enable the group to speak. I found a scrap of paper, took what I understood from the others' fragments of thought and in the back seat of that Peugeot began to write. I did not analyze at the time or even wonder why I could do it.

Later I realized that I had training, not adequate for the moment, but at least an appropriate education. I was a journalist. I had learned from simple class assignments to sift through a pile of confusion and pick out the reliable information. I had practiced leaving out the irrelevant, including my own biases.

If my colleagues could give up what they desperately wanted and accept another assignment, I could make the sentences that broke my heart. Not only had I received some training in the means and the necessity of doing this, but I had experience. When I was merely eighteen years old I had written the news story telling factually, objectively, the truth, that one of my friends had accidentally killed the other. Twenty years later I had been to the Allenby Bridge to meet refugees fleeing their homes now in the Israeli occupied West Bank. I was the one framing questions for the traumatized. I heard them, picked out bits of the truth and found the story behind their disorderly words, behind their fear of speaking the unspeakable and their explosive need to speak.

I had then written and sent to readers in the U.S. stories they did not want to hear.

In Lebanon through years of civil war and even invasions by neighboring countries, I had been press representative for the mission. Whatever happened to us, I was the one who had to organize it into something understandable on the other side of the world. With good news and bad, I had driven to a post office and filed reports to headquarters on a telex machine, while booms reverberated through the surrounding hills.

Now devastated and in a strange country, I was no stronger or wiser, no smarter or saner or calmer than anybody in this heartbroken group of people. But I had taken the training and done the job. I could make a few reasonable sentences stating our case.

Ursula LeGuin pointed out in one of her wonderful essays that childhood is about gaining, old age about losing. I didn't like that at the moment I read it. But, I have to admit it is true, that I am losing something, several things, maybe things I haven't even missed yet.

I had lunch out with Nancy and Eileen one day and while we were waiting for our food, a couple stopped by our table to greet me. They were people I had been quite friendly with a few years before, so we bantered back and forth about a fun experience, involving her birthday. I had seen him at the post office on that remembered day and he had told me he was taking her out to dinner in the evening.

I had asked if he had a gift, and he said, "No. I guess I need one, don't I."

And I said, "There's a pair of earrings she really wants. I can take you to see them."

Leaning over our table at the restaurant, he told me (I had heard it before) how totally impressed she had been by this perfect gift.

And while he talked, I was desperately searching my brain for these people's names, while poor Nancy and Eileen were sitting there ignored, surely feeling my rudeness in not introducing my friends.

Of course, I remembered, an hour too late. This is a big loss—the names of my friends, even if temporary. It makes me feel foolish, and I hate feeling foolish.

But, listen Ursula, it is not all about losing, because while I am losing some things I am also gaining some others.

I remember rather clearly being aware back when I was twenty-something that I never quite got the big picture. Didn't even have time to think about it. Life was a jumble of details, most of them things I didn't know and needed to learn. Everything I did then was a lesson in how.

How do you put together being a student and getting married? How do you make strawberry jam? How do you know when to take the baby to the ER?

Years later, in the Middle East, trying to publish Christian literature in the Arabic language, we were constantly undertaking something we did not really know how to do. The first Greek-Arabic Concordance ever, the only Bible Atlas in the Arabic language, the first indigenous church curriculum, a comprehensive hymnbook adding songs composed in our churches to great inherited hymns, with no software for printing the notes.

Occasionally, when we got discouraged, I would say to my staff, "The good thing is that when we get it done, we will know how."

And we did. On occasion we taught others. Groups came from other countries to take lessons from our editors in the creation of indigenous curriculum.

But we had learned, I found, a great deal more than the how-to's of literature development and production. We had learned how to ignore our excuses and just do it.

In the middle of a civil war we did it.

Thinking all of this made me feel better about Zach, even better about being old.

And I knew what my mother meant. When she was sitting there in her rocker, crippled by arthritis, I had quizzed her about a lot of things related to my childhood. And she told me stories. For instance, about Mr. White, the Singer Sewing Machine salesman. He called on my mother one day, bringing a sewing machine he said she needed. This was in the early thirties. Mother had three little girls and barely enough money to buy groceries. She had turned the back yard into a garden and a little chicken yard, from which she fed us vegetables and an egg most days. Only on Sundays when Daddy was home did we have meat.

Clothes were an issue. Barely literate enough, she could order from the Sears Roebuck catalog, but money to pay was the issue.

She told Mr. White that she could not have the sewing machine, because she could not pay for it. Mr. White told her in real terms how much money the machine would save her. She said she knew, but still, she didn't have money to pay for the machine. He gave her terms, a few dollars per month. But she didn't have those few dollars, she told him.

And Mr. White said, "Then sew fast, Mrs. Anderson, because I am going to leave this machine with you for a month. Then I will have to come and get it."

She scrounged materials, flour sacks, a few pieces from the dry goods store, and she sewed fast, learning to use the machine as she went, thinking all the time. And when Mr. White came, she said, "I will take it." She had skimped at the grocery store and sold some eggs. She thought she could do it.

After that Mr. White came monthly to collect, and she always had the money.

I went to school dressed as well as anybody and better than many. At our house we looked down our noses at "store bought" clothes. They never fit perfectly and came apart at the seams.

About the time I was talking with Rob about the deplorable failure of the Army and remembering stories my mother told me, I had accepted responsibility for a Sunday morning sermon in our little Methodist church. The pastor would be away; we had just one official lay speaker who would not be available. I am the bottom of the barrel, a little old and moldy.

So I put together a message on how we, by disciplining our own thoughts, can promote peaceful relationships and calm hearts. I used Philippians 4:8, the key words of which had been in front of me on my tack board for maybe a year, while I hoped to absorb their wisdom through some subliminal magic. (It seemed logical that if I had to prepare a lesson it should be one I needed.)

In the final step of my preparation I made a print-out of my notes, the cues I needed to be sure I mentioned the eight key words in this crucial sentence:

Whatever is true,

noble,

right,

pure,

lovely,

admirable,

anything excellent

or praiseworthy,

think about such things.

I wrote after each of the eight words just short phrases to remind me of my thoughts, with an occasional sentence I wanted to read. It all made several pages, because I printed it in a large font, so that I could see each point at a glance.

I thought I was ready.

Then on Sunday morning, before I had my clothes on, the telephone rang. My son Dwight, a man in his fifties, had suffered a stroke. He was nauseated, unable to see, his eyeballs rolling around in his head. Saying no to the idea of an ambulance and unable to walk, he had crawled to the car. His wife had taken him to the ER, which transferred him immediately to a hospital in Sacramento.

This was his second stroke; the first had left no damage, and we had hoped there would never be another.

I managed to eat something and put on my clothes. Half an hour before I needed to go to the church, I sat down with my printed notes and could not even read them. They were a jumble of words, mere symbols, cues to what, I couldn't remember.

When I got to the church, I asked the liturgist to please do everything—the readings, the prayers, the offering, so I didn't have to remember anything but my sermon. And I told no one about Dwight. I thought that if I asked for prayers, then people might be thinking about me when I stood up to speak, and that was not why they were there.

And I got up and did it. That's all I know. When the time came, the words made sense to me. Each point was clear. I said what I meant to say, read what I meant to read.

Afterwards, immediately, I drove to the hospital.

It was the end of the day when I realized that delivering the message had been a test of whether or not I could do the first thing it instructed: to think only what I knew to be true.

This is what I mean, Ursula. This is what my mother meant.

While learning to sew beautifully, doing something to be proud of, she also learned inadvertently what she could do when there didn't seem to be a way. She summed it up when she said, "I just do it."

Me, too. All my life I have been collecting evidence. I have been acquiring skills, discovering resources, practicing stubbornness. I am even beginning to see the big picture of who I am.

This is true of all of us elderly people. Though we have never before been exactly where we are right now, we have no reason to be afraid. We own storehouses we can open and find the tools, the expertise and the strength to deal with whatever comes. We have a wealth of experience in doing what we don't know how to do. Half our world collapses and we go on.

We are trained soldiers.

Everybody who is eighty-eight has eighty-seven years of practice.

We will just do it.

Zach sent me a picture of himself, stuffing his face with chocolate oatmeal peanut butter cookies. Maybe the Army has decided just to depend on grandmas.

I Will Give Myself a Break

Only recently have I realized that not everything I think about the past is true. Sometimes there is another way to tell our own story. In fact, I am a story-teller; I know that there is more than one way to tell almost any story and ways to tell a true story and leave out information. There are no alternative facts but there is partial information, and often mysteries are revealed by the apparent truths. And then there are different ways to see the facts. Different points of view create alternative ways to tell the story and lead to varying interpretations.

When my daughter Jan was three years old, this happened to us. I had put her to bed for an afternoon nap. Then I sat down in front of a television program I wanted to see. This was as close as I could come to taking a rest, because I had a toddler at my feet and a baby on my lap.

Jan got up and came to the little group in front of the television. She came dragging a small cardboard box. I asked her to go back and rest in her bed. She was not in a happy mood. She said she didn't feel like taking a nap, and while she talked she was scratching on the flap of the cardboard box with some instrument in her hand. I tried to follow the story on television. I had Jim playing at my feet. I was feeding baby Dwight.

Jan suddenly screamed and covered one eye with her hands. An instrument fell to the floor. A compass, the kind with two arms, a pencil on one arm for drawing a perfect circle, with the sharp point on the other arm, meant to hold the middle of the circle. And she held both hands over her left eye.

I don't know what I did immediately with the baby. I just remember looking into that beautiful brown eye and seeing a mark, a greyish disturbance in the middle of the pupil. I remember my whole body suddenly cold as though plunged into ice water.

I would give half my life to undo that one minute of our lives, but God does not accept human sacrifice nor undo what has been done. My precious little girl had lost an eye while sitting three feet from me. I had known with some part of my mind what she was doing, and I did not stop her.

The local doctor, horrified, picked up the phone and called someone. He said, "I am sending you a little girl who has stabbed herself in the eye." We went, Jan and I. She would not lie down in the car. She said, "No, Mommy, because if anything beautiful goes by, I want to see it."

How, in heaven's name, could a three-year-old say something so poetically and terrifyingly appropriate to the moment? Just after that we passed an orange tree in bloom, and I had the impulse to stop, but the doctor had told me to hurry.

There is no end to this story. It didn't just follow us through life; it evolved, it grew. Damage to an eye just keeps happening. For years we covered the other eye, trying to coax vision from the damaged one, all in vain. By the time she was six the eye was blind except she could see light, tell the difference between night and day, see car lights coming from her left. At eight she began to wear glasses because even the other eye was not strong. Twice the blind eye turned and we put her through surgery to correct her appearance. In adulthood after a small jolt, her car being hit from behind at an intersection, even the light went away. The already fragile retina had detached. Repair was not even worth the effort.

When she was in her fifties, the eyeball ached most of the time. Her doctor prescribed antibiotics for a low grade inflammation that just kept hanging on, and the eye seemed to shrink because it was sinking into its socket. Doctors said there was no way to save it; they would remove the eye and replace it with a prosthetic.

I traveled from California to Roanoke, Virginia to be with her for the surgery and take care of her during recovery. I got on the plane in California not feeling well, endured a delay in Philadelphia, flew to Lynchburg when the plane to Roanoke was canceled, was met at midnight by my grandson and driven to Roanoke, arriving with pneumonia.

I was especially disappointed to be unable to get up and go to Jan's church, Christ Episcopal, because that day they were having a special ceremony, anointing her with oil and praying for her healing. But afterwards, she brought oil home to do the same for me. She sat on the side of my bed and talked about my illness but even more about the event for which I had carried blame all those years. She told me that it was time for that wound to heal. She said, "I am letting it go, and I want you to let it go."

She put the oil on my forehead and prayed for me. And a great unexpected peace entered my heart.

Since then I have realized for the first time that the story I remembered, the way I always told it to myself, was only half true. In the first place, we were adding another room onto the house, temporarily compromising the space where the children slept. That dangerous instrument had been on a desk in that room. Such an instrument should never be in a children's room. It was not my compass, nor had I ever used it, nor did I put it there. I was a tired young woman who had recently given birth. It was my rest time, too, and I was just trying to have a few moments of adult relaxation. Jan was only three and her mother's attention had been stolen already by two little brothers. That was not fair to her or to me.

This more objective way of telling the story came to me only in the past year. And I tell it now, not to blame anyone else, but to tell the truth that my responsibility is not the whole story, and I never meant to neglect my child.

This is an example of what I mean when I say that I will give myself a break. In many situations in my life, I did not do the perfect thing. I was wrong; I made mistakes; I dropped the ball.

This one hurts the most.

Now that I am eighty-eight I can see the whole thing, but I have to do this over and over, partly because damage to this eye continues to cost. Six years after that drastic surgery to remove the eye, the eye socket required injections to lift the sinking prosthetic. More pain, more expense, more emotional trauma.

I am sorry, so always sorry that this happened. I am sorry for my part, even though I have received Jan's forgiveness, and God's. I know that if some other mother were telling this story, I would try to help her give herself a break. There is another way to tell the story, a way that shows that at the brief moment of this dreadful accident I was doing the best I could.

When Jan was a college student she asked me to write to her the story of what happened to her eye, and very late in life I have learned that she then blamed herself, that little three-year-old person, for being naughty, not going to bed when she was told!

Old age is surely easier if we don't let the errors of our youth weigh us down. Now at the point when whatever sense my life makes should become obvious, I need to tell myself the whole truth and give myself credit.

A partial truth is not yet the truth. Perhaps this explains why God, who knows the whole of all stories, is so astonishingly merciful.

I Will Forgive

This day should have been wonderful, a day with no appointments, no scheduled interruptions in the writing to which I meant to devote myself. But it began badly, because of mistakes I made last night.

First I ignored the clock and dawdled at everything I did in the evening. Without purpose or discipline I did whatever moved me at the moment, taking my own sweet time. When the evening news was over, I left the television on, let it make useless noise. I changed the channel once, not liking the twang of country music, and then again because I didn't want to think about crime. What I learned from all of that distraction was only that the Lakers beat the Trailblazers.

The good thing that happened came in my email, a letter from a dear friend, which I answered immediately, but because I was tired this went slowly, and because I saw today as wide-open and free, I did not concern myself about bedtime. In short, I stayed up too late.

According to my evening routine I took an antihistamine, a sleep aid and half a tablet of the medicine that helps to keep my heart steady. I almost took the anti-acid pill that I need most nights, but I am trying to wean myself away from that and decided that my supper had been innocent enough and I could do without it.

Getting under the covers after 11:00 I read Billy Collins poems until I was impossibly sleepy.

At shortly before five I woke feeling terrible. I had a headache. I thought maybe I was too hot. When I threw off some cover, I changed my mind. Then I noticed the burning in my throat. I realized I would have to take that pill after all. This required turning on the light. Back in bed, I decided that I should have taken also a Tylenol, so I got up again.

Then I lay awake. A lot of time went by, during which the devil got busy in my idle mind. Without knowing how or why it came back to me, I was remembering the beautiful quilt that my mother made for me. I can't describe the pattern, just the gentle pastel colors; I saw it only once.

For a period of time I had been alone in Lebanon, a country torn by divisions and violence, while Wayne supervised a building project for the mission in Jordan. (We had this problem all of the years we spent in the Middle East; whatever country we were in, another one wanted him.) Then I had come to the States for a brief period and was packing a crate to send to Lebanon. I had bought a lightweight coat, the style we called a car coat. I had purchased by the case a couple of things we loved to eat and could not buy in Lebanon. And I had done my Christmas shopping, exulting over the opportunity to be generous with my family with gifts from America. I don't remember what I bought for Dwight and Cynthia, the only two still with us, but I had bought Wayne a calculator. Calculators were new and expensive. Wayne was record keeper for the publishing house I directed, and he needed this for his work, but the calculator would be his. I had investigated thoroughly; it was the best personal calculator on the market.

Altogether I had a thousand dollars' worth of things in that crate, all important to our family. And then Mother gave me the quilt. So American, so authentic, artistic, beautiful, such a work of love. She was old already, her fingers becoming crippled with arthritis, and she had worked for a year, cutting and sewing. Her friends had helped her do the quilting. I knew I would treasure it for the rest of my life. And I put it into the crate.

The day I received notice that the crate had arrived in the Beirut port, I went to the office of a man who had handled for me numerous shipments of books out of the country. He told me that he would need my husband's passport in order to clear the crate through customs. This no doubt needs some explanation. The truth is that married women are often not permitted to speak for themselves in the Middle East and other places, even here. I could speak for the publishing house but not for myself.

I frequently flew to Amman to spend the weekend with him. On this occasion I went early to tell Wayne that he needed to appear in Lebanon on a work day and immediately, to clear the crate and have it delivered to the seminary where I was living temporarily in the guest apartment.

While he went, I stayed in Amman, expecting him to be back for the weekend. To my great surprise he came back the same day. Having left on the first morning flight, he was back by mid-day, saying that all the shipper had needed was his passport information. He had given him that with instructions where to deliver it, and he had gotten on the next plane back to Jordan.

Immediately I knew what would happen. I felt sick.

I told Wayne, "We will never get it."

He poohed at that, unconcerned.

I told him he needed to go back and let the shipper know he was there and waiting. He considered that silly. I said, "Wayne, in Lebanon, someone will loot your house now if you leave it for a period of time. The war has left many people in need and willing to get what they want any way they can get it."

I could not persuade him to go back.

I became angry, convinced that he was being just plain irresponsible. I could not understand his unwillingness to spend one day getting this crate into his possession.

On Monday I went back to Lebanon as planned. The crate was sitting in a logical place. I lifted the lid. It was empty.

Never in all these years have I hurt for the practical, purchased things that were in that crate. But I have grieved for my mother's quilt. I could never tell her what happened. And this need for silence caused me not to mention again how much I loved it, how much I appreciated her thoughtfulness and sacrifice.

This morning I realized that I never forgave Wayne for his nonchalance about a thing no one but he could do. It still eats at me. I can't find a way to justify his behavior.

The problem is that I buried the incident long ago. Apparently I buried it alive. I did not remember it for years, and now it has come back.

This morning I visualized a group of men, gleefully pilfering my crate. My anger flared up again. I remembered going to that businessman, the agent, and telling him that the crate was empty. And I saw that he knew. Instantly, he said, "Oh, that happened up there," meaning up at the school where they had delivered it.

I told him, "It did not happen there. You know what happened, and you know why you will never again get any work from me. I can find someone else to ship my books."

I left and never saw him again. I did not forgive him.

I will bet that he has forgotten, that it has never disturbed his sleep.

Wayne never asked me to forgive him. I don't think he ever understood what I lost. He let it go. I let it go. Against all the rules we know for harmonious living and pure hearts, we let it go.

Now here I am, alone with this problem.

In my Bible study class one day Mary Ellen said, "When we hold resentments, we hurt only ourselves. The people we are mad at go right on. They don't feel a thing."

She is right, of course. I am a perfect illustration of the principle.

Today, before the sun goes down, I must confess this to God, who already knows all. I must plead for help. I must find a way to pull this story up by its roots.

When I wrote a tentative outline for this manuscript, I vowed before I die to forgive every fault, every wrong, not thinking when I vowed of this one that arises now, destroying my sleep and threatening to destroy my day. I must find a way.

How do you forgive someone who is gone, having never confessed the need of it? This is hard.

What I know to do is to try to see the situation from his point of view.

He had not been there in Lebanon to feel the change that had taken place during months of war, the new climate of lawlessness, the breakdown of morals. (When your neighbors are killing one another, and your house has been hit with a shell, what's the big deal if you take someone else's calculator and quilt?)

But mostly, I imagine, that Wayne's mind was on his job in Jordan. He was supervising a building project and had caught the contractor putting an excessive amount of sand into the concrete walls. He needed to be present and responsible. So he gave the shipping agent what he said he needed and came back on the next plane.

And having never seen the things in that crate, he never missed them. They were just "things" to him. He never gave much importance to "things."

He was, after all, a kind and thoughtful man. His behavior that day was uncharacteristic. Probably that's why I didn't know how to handle it.

And it was not a deliberate wrong, just a bad judgment. I happen to know that it is really hard to be right all the time.

So he was not perfect. Big news! No matter how much we like to praise the dead, dying hasn't made them perfect. But to accuse them now is unjust; they cannot defend themselves.

I hope that when I am dead no one will sit around remembering what an insensitive dummy I was now and then.

Whatever Wayne was thinking on that distant day is now God's concern, not mine. So I am letting it go.

Already I feel how trivial this is, what a minor issue in the story of my life.

I Will Tell Stories

There are stories that matter, stories that tell the truth about me and my generation. I need to remember them, because I want to find their meaning, to understand, to know what difference my existence has made. The meaning is all in my stories.

When I was a child I had no books in my home.

Is this important?

I don't know. I think so. Probably.

Reasons I know well: when people need money for food, they don't buy books. That has to be one reason.

My mother was semi-literate with only a fourth grade education. She did not know what I was missing. That's another.

Since there were no books, and anyway, because my mother did not read fluently, no one read to me when I was a child. There was no bedtime story, no concept of a bedtime story.

When I went to school, I failed my first opportunity to learn to read. Is there a relationship between this and not having any books at home? I don't know, but I think so.

At the end of each school day our teacher read to the class the next day's lesson while we followed in our "readers." When I got home I still knew the words and could "read" the pages to my mother.

I fooled my mother. I fooled my teacher. I fooled myself. I believed that I was reading.

Then we arrived at the vocabulary list on the last page of the book. I can still remember a cloudy column of meaningless type and my confusion. How strange that some people could look at this list and see words!

So, what does this have to do with anything? How is it significant to my story?

I grew up to be a writer and a publisher. I led a community of Christians to create literature they needed.

How can this be explained?

What difference did it make that I had no books in my home, that I was too poor to own books, or that I had difficulty learning to read?

What influence did that have on my life?

I know the facts. I may not know the meaning of the facts. The meaning is like that hazy column of type in the back of my first reader.

The mystery of it all I recognize, the illogic between the beginning and the end.

One of these random facts startled me the other day, rising like a ghost out of a tomb to say, "Remember me?"

With the memory came a creepy feeling of shame. This, I realize is why I let myself forget.

The year was 1951. That is important.

I had enrolled in Golden Gate Baptist Seminary in Berkeley with the intention of studying the Bible and deepening my spiritual life. I had already a degree in journalism which I now saw as a tool. I was equipped to write, not just anything, of course, but clear, concise, factual news, and even to some extent opinions and little essays about people. I needed another subject, something that would add content to what I had to offer, something like history or economics or sociology. I was really reaching, I think, for something spiritual. I don't remember having any clear vision of how this could become my writing specialty; I suspect that I really just wanted it for myself. I had a hunger to understand the Christian scriptures more deeply.

The happy circumstance that enabled me to go to California and study was that Golden Gate needed me. They needed a student they could hire to assist the public relations director, and to take his place after a year. This enabled me to pay my bills while I studied the Bible. Or so, I thought.

On registration day I was surprised to discover that basically there were two tracks of study. One track was biblical and ministry courses. The other was religious education. The first was for men who planned to be pastors. The second was open to men and women. All of the women students were being enrolled in the latter, and, as it happened, no men at Golden Gate had chosen to study religious education.

On registration day, though this information was a surprise it did not seem critical. I was there; I was a seminary student. It was all good.

But a few days of my classes revealed the fact that my courses were not what I really wanted. I was studying the church organizations: the Sunday School, the training and mission organizations. We would have in the first semester just a survey of the Old Testament, and then a survey of the New Testament. These were broad, introductory courses, in the same class with men who were also first year students. The deeper courses required Greek and Hebrew and were not open to women students.

The professors were fascinating, especially the Old Testament teacher, but for some reason (odd to me that first time) he announced two assignments for private study: one for men, the other for women. The one assigned to the men was the one that appealed to me, because it required them to dig deeply into the meaning of certain passages of scripture.

So, very shortly I decided to go to the registrar and say that I did not want to study Religious Education, because I really wanted the other track, the one that took the student into the study of scripture itself.

The registrar, Dr. Manning, was an approachable man, easy to talk to, with a practical mind. But when I got to his office, he did not happen to be there. His secretary (maybe she was his assistant, but I understood at the time that she was just a secretary) sat behind a desk in an outer office. She asked why I needed to see Dr. Manning, so I told her.

Immediately she informed me, her voice scandalized, that I could not do that. Those courses were for men, because the men would preach and become pastors of churches.

Though I don't remember now the words she used, I know she made me feel that I had aspired to a privilege improper for a woman. I had no right to those courses. My asking implied that I wanted to usurp the rightful place of a man.

The idea of standing behind a pulpit and preaching as my pastors had done since I was a child had never crossed my mind. I was stunned and embarrassed that my request carried this false implication, and I left that office and never told this story to anyone.

Julie, Sterline, Betty and I, all beginning students, became so close that we remained friends for life and traveled great distances to be together again with our husbands, but I never told them that I had wanted to study what the men studied. At the beginning I suspected that those three were smart enough to know that what I had done was unthinkable. And then I pushed it out of my mind so far that I never thought of it again when we were together.

Now I wonder, did any of them have the same wish I had? If we had talked about it, would we have gotten courage to go together and ask? I also wonder what Dr. Manning would have said to me, if he had been there that day. I suspect that he would have, at least, been kinder. He might have explained that the seminary had a policy, and he had to abide by it. But maybe not, because in 1964 when we arrived in Lebanon and met our colleagues, we learned that Mabel Summers had been the first woman to get the degree the men took at

Southern Seminary in Louisville, Kentucky. If Mabel could, why couldn't I?

The world was changing. I wish I had realized that and pushed a little harder on the closed doors.

I can't say that the seminary course I took was of no value. What I learned about teaching the various ages and about the ethos of the different educational organizations in churches was worthwhile afterward in two churches that Wayne pastored before we went abroad. And of course that background was valuable when I led the Baptist churches of the Middle East in the creation of their own indigenous church curriculum.

Fast forward now twenty-four years to 1975. Having come home from Lebanon for a summer furlough, we had gotten stuck in California when war in Beirut made it impossible to get back to our home. Wayne and I were invited to speak in a Baptist church on a Sunday evening. At least that's what we thought. Maybe the invitation had been intended for Wayne only.

Arriving early, we sat on a front pew until the pastor came and greeted us warmly and wanted to talk about the evening's program. In the conversation that ensued Wayne explained that he would speak first in a general way about ministries in Lebanon; then I would tell about the work of the publishing house, because I was the director. The pastor seemed surprised, though he made an effort to hide his surprise, and a few minutes afterward there was a flurry of activity as men came, bringing wires and a microphone and set them up just in front of us.

Then, with the congregation gathering, the pastor asked Wayne to come up to the platform and sit beside him, explaining that I could simply stand up where I was and use the microphone that had been prepared. Though I realized immediately that I was not welcome in the pulpit, I liked the ease of sitting unobtrusively on the front pew and not needing to be on the platform.

Wayne said that he would also like to stay where he was.

The pastor said, But I want you on the platform with me, and Wayne said, I like being here with my wife.

But, the pastor said, you need to speak from the pulpit. And Wayne, courteously and quietly, said that he preferred to speak wherever his wife spoke.

I don't know what any of the people who observed this understood from it, but the pastor, unless he was especially obtuse, got the point. If I could not stand in that pulpit, neither would Wayne.

I loved him outrageously at that moment.

One reason to tell stories is that stories remembered reveal me to myself. I see it now: there at Golden Gate in the registrar's office: a little flame burning in the core of my being, wrapped in the asbestos of my time in history. Telling it, I see it from outside, and understanding erases the shame.

At crucial moments of my adult life I remembered

the poverty of my childhood. It was impossible not to see myself in Arab children. There was so little literature for them, and that is my definition of poverty. I don't remember being hungry, except for books.

Once in Damascus we went to a familiar shop on the street called Straight, looking for a certain artisan's beautiful boxes of inlaid wood. Knowing that the owner of the shop had several children I took a handful of story leaflets with me that day. We had to park some distance from the shop and walk in the heat of Damascus, heat that sucks the moisture out through your pores. It makes your feet heavy, your eyeballs dry, your head light and dizzy. The shopkeeper/artist was happy to see us, and right away began taking boxes off the shelves to show us the variety of designs.

A boy was there, maybe a ten-year-old, in a long striped robe like his father's, so I handed him a leaflet, just one folded sheet with a colored picture on front and a Bible story inside. He rewarded me with a quick smile and left, and in a couple of minutes there was a rush of children, a little bunch with eager hands, looking for a story, and after all my leaflets were gone, one little boy, with a pinched face, who burst into tears, because there no more stories.

The way I felt was maybe a little unreasonable. Other children could have shared with him, but his heartbreak was more than I could bear. I left Wayne to choose boxes and trudged back through the cluttered, dusty streets, with the sun burning my fair skin, to find the car and get another story.

Only a few months after I became director of the small Christian publishing house in Beirut, I faced a painfully difficult problem. Our small staff, hired to do the various jobs related to creating, publishing and selling books, was also running a lending library. The library had been established by my predecessor who had actually established the institution. She was an especially loved member of our "mission," a group of Americans working in Lebanon. Virginia was a brilliant woman, fluent in Arabic, a thinker, an innovator, a quiet person with a big heart.

She had established as an arm of the publishing ministry a library especially for young people, and in order to do this she had planted the publishing house in a Muslim community called the Basta where the library would be available to the youth of that community. And she had moved herself into an apartment several floors up from the library.

The venture had been successful as a gesture of good will. The book shelves included the texts needed by high school students to prepare for government exams, and the community was grateful. The Lebanese society was in need of things that created friendship between people of different religions, so support for the library had grown rapidly, until one night someone threw a fire bomb through the window from a passing car. The explosion awakened the neighborhood and brought people out of the apartments to fight the fire. Some were heard to say, "Shame! This is for our children."

Most of the books were saved, but damage had been done. Stories in the papers. A summons to Virginia from the Minister of Interior who told her that Lebanon was on the verge of civil war and he didn't think she wanted to be the spark that started a conflagration.

Virginia had gone to the man's office with one arm bandaged and in a sling. She had had a patch of melanoma removed, and this was not the first. Heartbroken, she went home, locked the library, and put a "Closed" sign in the window.

It was Virginia's death at the age of forty-two that created the vacancy that I was trying to fill. There had been an interim director who moved the office, and with it the library, to a safer area. Slowly, slowly, the youth of the Basta were venturing out of their familiar streets to get to the books they needed. And the existence of the library brought various other people, including adults in the new neighborhood, who loved to sit and read and converse with my obliging staff. Consequently, the staff was busy with people, helping them find books, recommending, and even counseling people with problems and questions. Getting our primary job done—planning, translating, writing, editing, proofreading—was becoming more and more difficult.

I perceived that there were two ways this library was not our duty. First, it was an anomaly administratively, because it was a purely local work, and the publishing house was an international ministry with an international board. Secondly, checking out books and having long conversations with visitors was not related to publishing or the actual job descriptions of people who were doing it.

Consequently I proposed to sell the library and get down to work publishing books. The board understood and approved, but my staff objected, expressing their opinion by dragging their feet about implementing and shifting their eyes away to avoid talking about the issue. Finally, they voiced their opposition, "This is not what Miss Cobb would do."

In my office I had a picture of Miss Cobb on my wall. She stared at me as I sat in "her" chair, where I often squirmed and wrestled with the sense of injustice and inappropriateness of my being there in "her" place. Day after day I questioned God and tried to understand why He had let this happen. The only answer I ever got from this questioning was the reality. I was there now, commissioned to do this job. And I could live my own life, but not Virginia's.

I called a meeting of the staff and I told them, "I have bad news for you. Miss Cobb is not coming back. I am responsible for this work. I can't, every time I have a decision to make, ask myself, 'What would Miss Cobb do?'"

I made it plain that I was supposed to be running an international publishing house, and that's what I planned to do.

That's the day when I turned the work around to grasp its real purpose. I sold the library to a school whose director was thrilled to get it. I instructed editors to stay in their offices and let the receptionist handle visitors. Starting that day the publishing house began to turn out books and develop its market.

For twenty-four years I did what I was prepared to do and built a publishing house that stands until today.

Next to the story of going to Sunday School when I was three and discovering the love of God, this is perhaps the most significant story from my life. But I realize this and tell it now only because I am coming to the end and need to understand what I have done with these years. Faced with explaining somehow my longevity in such a dangerous world, I can only say what happened. I do not claim to speak for God. I can admit the circumstance: before Virginia was taken away, God had prepared someone, me, to step into the role. I was there with some relevant training, a vision, and a willingness.

Christian scripture says that we are saved by God's grace, not because of anything we have done, but in the same breath claims that we are created for the good work that God has prepared in advance for us to do.

Yet I have difficulty saying that God protected me from every hazard to keep me for His purposes, no matter how obvious it seems, because there is still Virginia, looking down at me from the wall of our shared history. What about her and her marvelous gifts, wiped out after half a chance? Was there not room for both of us?

I have found no way to boast of what God has done for me. I can only say that I did with pleasure and with all my might the work that fell to me, my own assignment.

The grandmothers in my life are powerful images.

One with leathery skin, in a shapeless dress, bringing cornbread out of the wood stove, bread that smelled basic, like toasted grain, like the answer to all hunger. She cut it at the table and distributed great yellow, steaming chunks into our bowls where we crumbled it, burning our fingers, and she poured in milk, still warm from the cow.

Later she closed the shutters, lighted the lamps, laid pallets on the floor and hung over them filmy white tents to keep the mosquitoes out.

One of my young uncles killed and skinned a squirrel that she boiled with spices and rice into a delicious Louisiana jambalaya.

Mother called her "Mama." I called her "Grandma."

She was a mystery with sunken eyes.

Another created beautiful dresses, guiding cloth under the needle while she peddled her sewing machine. She claimed her eyesight had gotten better with age. She stood up so straight, she seemed to have a board for a back.

When I left books from the university library lying around the house they disappeared into her room. She hoped I could renew them, because she had not quite finished.

She was a Baptist, but she really liked the pope.

She told me once that there had been many huge changes in the world in her lifetime, but, she predicted, the changes in mine would be much greater.

I knew that she had been widowed with five young children, had sold the farm and moved to town so that she could make a living. So many questions come to me now about what that was like, how she grew little boys into men and sent some of them to college just making evening gowns, but I never asked, and she never told.

She would not tell me how old she was. Rather, she told me never to ask a lady her age.

Her discipline was legendary. She never needed an alarm clock; if she needed to get up an hour early one morning, she would just tell herself that, when she went to bed the night before.

Her face, her bearing, her walk, her way of working sent a message about dignity. One did not, in the face of foolishness, become foolish. Not one related to this lady.

My daddy called her "Mother." And my mother did, too. She was the only one I called "Grandmother."

The third was not related to me but was the one I knew best. That was Lola Ezell, who lived nearby, the one who taught my mother to cook and defended me when I was scolded for being a child. Just learning to talk, I called her Zell. And that is her name until now.

I remember that once she gave me a cookie with nuts in it. I was not accustomed to nuts in my cookies. Zell and Mother were seated at the kitchen table chatting while I circled the table, playing. Stopping beside Zell, I pulled her hand toward me and spit the nuts into her palm.

Mother was appalled, but Zell said, "She can spit nuts into my hand if she wants."

She was fat and talked all the time, on and on. She dipped snuff and in the middle of her rambling stories stopped to spit into a coffee can. She smelled bitter and sweet like the brown stuff in her can.

After her husband died and her son and daughter went away to work, Zell moved to the big city, to

Memphis to become the "linen lady" in a hotel. When I was ten I went there once, on the train by myself, and slept in her room with her in the double bed. In the drowsy dark she told me that she had always been jealous of my grandmother.

"Why?" I wanted to know.

"Because she's your grandmother, and I'm not." That was the first time an adult trusted me with a secret, something from the inside of their person. This is the first time I told anybody.

Much later in life I realized that Zell was complicated, and my daddy didn't like her. I was not sure why but felt disillusioned; it meant that my daddy, who was smarter than anybody, could still be wrong.

One thing makes me feel good. Just before Wayne and I sailed to the Middle East in 1964, we found Zell where she lived in Tennessee, and I took my husband and children to visit her. We adults sat in the backyard, drinking sweet iced tea, while the children chased "lightning bugs" and caught them in Zell's fruit jars, the way I did when I was a child.

The point now is that these three fascinating people were in my life and then not, and later, much later, all the questions came to me, all the unknown truths about their lives, their worlds, all the struggles and what they learned from them, the history that unfolded around them, all the things they knew that I don't and never will.

Now I see that they all failed me in this one way. They did not tell me their stories. Young people don't ask the elderly about their own history. Of course not! Young people don't question adults about the multiplication tables or how to be courteous to the neighbors; we teach them because they need to know and will be sorry later if they don't.

When they are sixty, after their grandparents are all buried, they will think to ask about their lives. Like Tom, the son of my friend Jim, who died unexpectedly in an accident, his wife already taken by a devastating disease. Now Tom, an orphan without a history, wants to know: in the old hometown, where was his grandpa's tinsmith shop? What were his father's parents like? What did they do that was interesting? Does anyone remember? Would they call? Or write and tell him?

Old people, before they get hit by a train or a heart attack, have to be responsible for passing on stories that explain themselves and their time, because eventually all our offspring will want to know where they came from and what they are carrying into the future.

That is the second reason I must tell stories.

I think there is a third.

When I was in Lebanon, where I had become a catalyst making this wonderful thing happen—Christian literature in the Arabic language—I wrote to my mother almost every week and she wrote to me. The real stuff of my life never got into those letters, because she was not prepared to understand what it was I did.

Nowadays I talk on the phone with Cynthia who is a manager at the Jet Propulsion Lab. Some days she has a small administrative problem that I understand, but how is she responsible for providing "tools," software tools and data systems to engineers who are designing, building and testing spacecraft to explore the universe? This I understand no better than my mother understood what in the world I was doing in the middle of a war in Beirut.

My story is about the wonder of how I got from there to here. I remember my embarrassment in the registrar's office, away back in the dark ages. I see it, side by side, with my pride now that my eldest daughter is an ordained minister and university chaplain.

But our story is only partly about us. It is about our world; the way we changed it, the way it changed us.

Our granddaughters have no clue unless we tell them.

Our grandchildren will not know the works of God in our lives unless we talk and write stories.

We are links, stretching out our hands, holding it all together—the people we came from, the people we send forth.

What My Scars Say

I recognize this, that I am scarred, but I am O.K. with it, sort of.

The neat thing about scars is that they always have a clear reason. Mine, every one, represents a story about something that happened to me in this dangerous world, though sometimes I hide them, scars and stories.

The oldest of these is a tiny mark from the nail through the first knuckle of my left pinkie, gained when I was so short I had to fully extend my arms to reach the table top where my mother was beating a tough piece of meat with a butcher knife. Both the mark and the memory are nearly invisible but somehow associated with a vision of my mother bursting into tears.

Because of the rather monstrous scar on the back of my left arm, a hole really, a deep hole several inches long, I don't like to wear a sleeveless dress. That story begins with a little lump, a hard knot that hurt when I leaned on it. It grew. My arm lost some flexibility. Soon I could not bend it enough to touch the back of my neck. We were living in Jordan. The doctor who tried to cut the lump away found tenacious roots. The plastic surgeon in Beirut, who hoped those roots were not fastened to the bone, tried to prepare me to lose my arm. I lost flesh, from my elbow a third of the way to my shoulder, and a layer of muscle, plus, temporarily, a thin slice of skin from my hip, used to make the graft on my arm.

I was still in my thirties with very young children. The sight of my arm scared them, but my sensitive six-year-old would not let anyone say it was ugly. With remarkable courage, she kissed it. Exercising it under hot water was not simple in the bathtub. The great wound healed; the doctor pronounced it "beautiful." With effort and time the arm learned to do its fair share, the left-handed share of a job for two hands. It still gets cold in autumn and needs a coat when the other arm doesn't, but the fibro sarcoma never came back.

Knowing I had lived in Jordan, an alert child in Lebanon thought I had been wounded by napalm in the six-day war. I gave her a hug, because she was close. (I was wounded by knowing a child with her eyelids burned off, but that scar is one I can usually conceal.)

Then there is my tummy, which looks like a battleground. Three surgeries, three stories, a couple more reasons I am still here. It is easy to die of cancer while nobody is looking in a country at war, with people bleeding to death on hospital steps. But friends stood in line to give me blood while others circled my bed to pray and doctors ignored gunfire to come to work. I don't often have to explain these criss-crossing lines, because I never did wear bikinis.

And maybe the curve in my back doesn't fit the common idea of a scar, but it is, for sure a mark imposed by experience. Of all my physical scars it is the hardest to love, the one that gets worse with time.

When I was nearly ten I got a little sister. Mother let me name her. She is Martha. For a couple of years she was my life. I fed her, changed her diapers, played "patty cake" with her little hands, rocked her to sleep. With no baby buggy, no stroller, I, a scrawny child myself, took Martha for walks in the sun, carrying her. She was a fat and beautiful baby, blue-eyed and blond. I had no need for dolls anymore; mine was real, alive.

She had measles, crying in misery, except when I was rocking her. Years later when my children had this hateful disease, I recognized it by the stale, musty smell. Some doctors don't know measles by the smell.

I heard our neighbor tell my mother, "That child is going to have a hump in her back from carrying that baby around."

What child worries about such things? Mother was always bent, over the wash tub or her garden. She didn't have a crooked back.

I was about twelve when we moved to another house on the edge of town, near a cotton field. Beside the field a small, unpainted house, was occupied by a share cropper, a sweet old man, black with a fringe of white hair. The segregated town had grown, encroaching on the surrounding fields, giving us this black neighbor. We kids loved him. I wish I could remember his name.

Ripe cotton, white clusters bursting out of the bolls, was a source of income for kids willing to work. On Saturdays I would go over and work all day, in the hot sun, bending over the plants, scratching my fingers on the edges of the bolls, while dragging the canvas sack that grew heavier with every step. Sometimes I worked for two hours after school, competing with myself for one penny more than yesterday. The old man trusted us to weigh the sack and tell him how much we had picked. He gave us a penny per pound.

When I was thirteen I was five feet eight, as tall as I would ever be. With no way of knowing that shrimpy eighth grade boys might become six feet with muscles, I did not want to stand up straight.

In college I had a boyfriend, a really nice young man, a poet with whom I sat around on Sunday afternoons listening to Tchaikovsky. My grandmother told me he was too short for me. She was five two or three and straight like a wooden soldier.

All my adult life, that slight bend just below my shoulders increased, slowly, slowly. It concerned my husband. He bought braces that never fit. He reminded me to hold my shoulders back. He taught me exercises designed to help. Taking care of my own five children didn't help, nor living with counter tops always a little low, but there is no excuse. Sometimes I was just too busy to pay attention. Wayne did not dislike me for it; he was trying to help.

It is a scar, I have decided. Not Martha's fault, not my mother's, partly mine maybe. But life happens and leaves marks.

One of the marvels of my scars is that not one is from a wound of war. None from shrapnel or flying glass or a sniper's bullet. So many dead and maimed, while the rest of us walked through fire and were never burned. Not a scratch on our skin. I can celebrate scars and the absence of scars.

Scars don't tell everything. They are just a body's memory of its own life.

But mine remind me of my erect and disciplined grandmother and my caring husband, of bending over the beautiful cotton and the patient, needy people who do backbreaking chores, of my hardworking mother and my dear little sister, and the smart, funny children God gave me. Of things I have done for love. Things I have survived. And a few things I lost on the way to winning.

Scars have a good purpose. I hide them when I can, but in my better moments I love them.

I Will Be Responsible for Health

When I woke yesterday morning, my body felt like a slug, barely willing to creep down the hall to the kitchen for my morning coffee. Then when I sat in my rocking chair, having forgotten to open the curtains so I could see the beautiful world, I thought, Why did I bother to get up?

This did provoke me to remember that I had work to do, and it happened that my responsibilities for the day were mainly mental. Great! Just when I felt like my head was full of mashed potatoes.

Thank goodness that was yesterday and is now behind me.

This morning was different. I got up earlier than I really had to, remembering a mid-morning phone appointment and the things I looked forward to talking about. Then when I sat down with my coffee, a bright idea came to me for another chapter of this book. I grabbed a piece of scratch paper and started scribbling, just to make sure the idea didn't get away before I could give it serious attention. This caused a rush of gratitude. Nothing makes me happier than a useful idea.

How do I account for the difference in these two days? It's easy. In fact, I probably have the explanation for Dr. Jekyll and Mrs. Hyde: a good night's sleep.

My energy, my creativity, my attitude, my productivity, my usefulness to the world, my practical age, all come down to this simple need for sleep.

The truth is that I have a couple of physical problems that often make sleep difficult. And I can't do anything about my propensity to these problems; they are part of my genetic makeup. Getting older has made them worse, just as it somehow makes my bad feet worse.

But the rest of the story is that there are certain things I can do to minimize the problems. Last night I took my supplements on time, according to the schedule I know works best. And I ate the right things in the afternoon and evening, unlike the day before. There are some recommended practices for preparing for bed, and last night I paid attention to these, profiting from the experience of others.

Today I get to reap the benefits of taking responsibility for my own well-being. This is not to say that I won't have health problems that I could not avoid. Of course I will. In fact, I still have those two issues that are hindrances to my sleep. They are not going away. Some nights they will win.

Bu they are my problems, not my children's, not my friends,' not the world's. And I have a choice: to be mad and show it by ignoring the facts I am saddled with, or take responsibility for myself.

Sometimes, not always, but often, doing what I know to do makes a big difference.

Today I am prepared for that phone call. I have made notes. I have written questions. I am wearing my hearing aids. I have paper on which to scribble answers. I have eaten breakfast and thanked God for the coming opportunities, known and unknown of this day. These are all signs that I slept almost enough last night.

Last year I was sick the first three months of the year. I had diarrhea so often, so badly, that trips out of the house were risky.

My GP took away some of my supplements, things that might have a laxative effect. My gastroenterologist ran tests that turned out negative, then decided that we must do the drastic thing, a colonoscopy to check for a particular kind of infection that can be found only by taking a sample from the wall of the colon.

Meanwhile at home, I started keeping a record of what I ate shortly before each episode of diarrhea and discovered that every time I ate leafy greens I had diarrhea the next day.

Leafy greens are my favorite vegetable. I love them all: collards, chard, kale, spinach, beet greens, turnip greens. And I had been finding these in my local grocery and eating them several times a week. I tried eliminating greens from my diet; I got better. I ate them again and got worse.

I called my gastroenterologist and told him the story. He commended me and said, "We don't want to do this colonoscopy if we don't really have to do it." And we never did it!

I keep getting better, except in response to those luscious greens. Sometimes I get away with eating small portions.

When I listen to my body, it tells me what is going on. I know it rather intimately and understand its language. When I am about to have a serious hypoglycemic meltdown, I feel it coming, and I grab a bag of nuts or a protein bar covered with chocolate.

Being responsible for my own health sometimes makes me stay at home. Sometimes it causes me to call the doctor and make an appointment. Sometimes it permits me to cancel an appointment with the doctor. Sometimes it tells me to get up from behind this computer and walk. That's the hardest thing. The longer I sit here the weaker I am, so the more I need to move, the less I want to.

I have established a summer time schedule for walking, a time when the heat eases off and part of the road is shaded. The more I have slept the night before, the longer I can walk. The more I walk, the better I sleep. It all works together. And I have some control.

Right now my body is telling me to turn off this computer, run a warm bath and get ready for bed.

I have two granddaughters who are wonderful examples to me. They suffer with psoriasis that makes ugly red patches on their skin, and there is no cure for this obnoxious problem. But they have learned to control the symptoms with medical treatment and diet.

Because it is not on her diet, Marissa watched the rest of us eat her birthday cake, the cake her mother chose to make because it is Marissa's all-time favorite.

She said, "Thanks, Mom. It looks wonderful," then sat there smiling, looking beautiful.

Lately ordinary housework gives me a pain in my lower back. Pushing the vacuum cleaner, leaning over to pick up yesterday's socks, pulling open a kitchen drawer, scrubbing the bathtub—I can do them all, but then I need to sit with ice or heat on my back. Worse yet, I feel like an old lady, and neither the ice nor the heat helps my feelings.

I have been talking to myself about this. Clearly I am losing core strength, but somewhere I have a set of exercises to help that. After thinking this for a couple of weeks, I got serious enough to search for that "somewhere" document of instructions. I emptied my file on health issues and leafed through numerous clippings and newsletters and finally found it. A great relief! I laid the paper out where I could see it and went back to whatever I had been doing a couple of hours before.

Only when I had another backache did I take note that finding the article had helped me not at all, just as having it in my file cabinet had never helped. I actually have to do the exercises. What a drag!

Reading the directions, I encountered the first problem immediately. These maneuvers require lying down on the floor. Is that smart? If I lie down on the floor, can I get up again? Of course I can; I get out of the bathtub. How do I do that? Hmmm . . . I think I make my arms do part of the work.

I found a place on the bedroom rug, near a chair that might be useful when I'm done.

I lay down with the directions in my hand and right away discovered that two of those maneuvers are off my radar. One needs a prop I don't have right now; the other is just beyond my physical ability. These have to be goals. The four I tried and could do made me hopeful. I did a few reps; better not to overdo and make something sore.

I rolled over onto my knees and got up, pushing a little with my right arm in the seat of the chair. Just getting on the floor and getting up again made me feel stronger and safer.

My physical well-being is a major element in my independence. If I want to stay in my house and keep doing the things I like to do, I need to be able to handle the day-to-day activities in some way. Not taking care of my health is a way of giving up, a plain signal that I am tired of the struggle and ready for someone else to take care of me.

In a brochure my postman delivered yesterday, Dr. Bruce Ferrell in the Division of Geriatrics at UCLA's David Geffen School of Medicine says that our genes account for thirty percent of how we age. "The remaining 70 depends on you."

Wow! I didn't expect, when I opened my mail, such powerful support for my own observation. That may send me down on the rug again.

I Will Keep Growing

A long time ago, more than fifty years in fact, we were living just outside a Jordanian village in the hills of Gilead, where we were part of a group of about eighteen Americans. My husband and two single women ran schools in the village, but most of the others were doctors and nurses in the only hospital in the area. In a regular business meeting of the group, whoever was responsible for the devotional that day asked us to think about what we would like to have written on our tombstones.

Yikes! What a question. Am I supposed to think about such things?

The question was passed around the room. There was a little stammering and some glibness. People expressed the wish to be considered loving, sacrificial, devoted, that kind of sentiment. I was one of the last to answer, because of where I was sitting in the circle. I didn't know what I would say, until it was my turn, and I had to say something.

I said, "She kept growing 'til the end."

As our friend Adrian Middleton once said in my presence, "I didn't know what I thought, 'til I heard what I said."

For sure I was talking to myself. No one else would remember what I said, just as I don't remember what they said.

But what I said has stuck with me.

It's possible that on that day in Jordan I was prone to mistake learning for growing. In my old age I realize the difference and have changed my emphasis.

I have decided finally to stop pursuing information for storing in my head.

I mean that, though honesty requires me to admit that my decisions don't always get enforced. As I read I still mark words I don't know, sometimes even stopping to look them up. I get a possible new word for my vocabulary in a daily email from Merriam-Webster, and I love it. I also permit trivia questions to arrive in my mail box, and it annoys me that I know so little about some things, for instance, the world's islands—what seas they are in, who owns them. Books still proliferate in my house, because I am interested in so many subjects, and every day I need some fact that I am not carrying around in my head.

Often I ask Google. What a boon! The amazing availability of information permits me to forget what I read, knowing I can ask again anytime. (Google never points out, as some people would, "I told you that yesterday.")

But I admit it is too late now to indulge all of my curiosity. I will never be a contestant on Jeopardy, so it seems useless to spend time stuffing trivia into my head. I flush a lot of unessential information without even thinking about it in busy, creative moments, but most days my curiosity wins. I want to know.

Nevertheless I have this straight in my head. When I talk about growing I am not talking about learning. The growing that seriously concerns me now is about changing, about becoming, about evolving at last into somebody better. I am concerned, not with what I know but with who I am.

Now I remember that years before that meeting in Jordan I was already concerned about this. Wayne was pastoring a little church in northern California. That made me a pastor's wife, in a position to see a lot of suffering, a lot of foolish living and some struggles to overcome errors made in the past. How to help all of these people who bared their souls to us, or in some cases just revealed themselves by their actions, was a pressing need.

In that period of time I thought it would be wonderful to be old, because then I would be wise. I would know life's secrets, how one could deal with the obstacles and griefs and become better because of them. I would know what to say, how to help.

Now I am eighty-nine and have known for a very long time that it is possible to be old and not wise.

Culture and religion have created artificial milestone years in people's lives. These seem to express hopes and possibilities more than realities. Kids get declared old enough to be responsible. They are "confirmed" by the church. They get a license to drive the family car, no matter the development of their brains. The right to an alcoholic drink, along with the privilege of dying for the country, is a reward for a couple more years of living. Not only that; at eighteen we are all legally adults, old enough to vote on issues relevant to survival of the planet.

Acknowledging that some legal line must be drawn, we all know that a genuine adult cannot be created by a birthday or a decree.

Or do we know that?

Here where I live in California there are laws relevant to this that really bother me. A juvenile can be considered an adult in court if he is accused of a really heinous crime. In other words, a fourteen-year-old, whose brain is not yet fully developed, (making him probably the only person who doesn't believe this) can make a sudden careless decision and kill somebody, and in order to punish him adequately, a district attorney can snap his/her fingers and declare him an adult. One moment he was a silly kid who disobeyed his mother and went out foolishly onto the dangerous street, and the next he is an adult, because we said so, and we want him to spend every single day of the rest of his life in prison protesting his death penalty.

This reminds me of a little story I read one time about children in kindergarten. They had some little animal in a cage; maybe a rat or a lizard. They wanted to give their cute friend a name. The naming process was fun until they realized that a lot of names carried connotations of maleness or femaleness, and they didn't know the sex of their pet. They did as much physical examination as they knew how without finding any clues and were completely stymied until somebody had a brilliant solution: "Let's take a vote."

I never found out what they decided. Nor did I cede to society the ability to define maturity.

What is a fully grown-up person? When do we get there, if ever?

One of the things I learned from living in foreign cultures is that the understanding of maturity varies around the world. For instance, as an American I tried to raise my children to be independent, strong individuals, able to think for themselves and accept responsibility for their own actions and the consequences. It was something of a shock for me to discover that in the Middle East people taught their children to depend on the family and consult their elders in all major decisions. This duty applied to the whole of their lives.

A young Arab man told me that choosing a wife was much too big a decision to make by himself.

The reason this whole subject is so important to me now is simply that I am looking at my last chance to be what I want to be, and I am not even totally sure what the goal is. It seems to move as I approach. I don't ever arrive at a place where I no longer need to keep growing.

This has seemed to require careful thought about what it is I hope to reach. Using the work of numerous teachers, delving into my own experience, thinking the best I know how, I have been able to write down for myself what I understand right now to be a mature person, a person I would like to be. I know it involves being responsible, humble, objective, disciplined, empathetic, sociable and spiritual. Of course, these are only categories, and there are various ways in which each is revealed. They are ideals, and the ideals might be directions, rather than destinations.

The really scary thing is that it is possible to regress in old age. I was devastated to learn this from my own mother. Not from her advice but from her sometimes shocking behavior.

When she was young Mother tended to be a quiet person, listening more than she talked. This seemed to be her humble nature.

When she was old she talked incessantly, to the extent that telling her anything became difficult. She did not listen. One could call her on the telephone to give her a message and never get the chance.

She didn't listen, because she couldn't hear. Thinking that she could not afford hearing aids, she decided that her problem was beyond the help of technology. She told us this for years, during which we did not know that her doctor begged to fit her with hearing aids.

Her way of handling telephone calls became also the method of dealing with face-to-face conversation. She was likely to interrupt a visitor with some irrelevant talk, leaving him looking stunned and the story he was telling dangling without conclusion.

I tell this only to illustrate the obvious way that a handicap can lead to thoughtless, rude behavior and worse.

Once I was with Mother and my sister Betty in Betty and her husband E.B.'s home in Louisiana. They had moved to this town a few weeks earlier, taking Mother with them.

It was early morning, and Mother and I were together in the living room, Mother in her wheelchair, when there came an urgent knocking on the door. I opened to an obviously agitated woman who asked for my sister. I invited her in and we stood there as I summoned Betty, who came quickly.

The visitor immediately described a crisis situation at her home and asked if E.B. could come and help her with it. Betty promised to send him quickly, and the woman left.

Mother promptly asked, "Who was that?" and without waiting for an answer, pronounced her, "the rudest person I ever saw. She stumbled in here, raving about who knows what, and ignored me as though I am not even sitting here."

Betty, in her patient way, pointed out that her visitor had not come to be sociable. She was in obvious distress, focused on her urgent purpose.

But Mother said, "Well, those people where you lived before, they always paid attention to me. They even asked about me when I was not in the room."

At the moment it was a mystery to me what happened to the humble, selfless mother who raised me.

I really want, now that I am old, to remember still that I am not the center of anybody's universe. Being handicapped, feeble and needy will not move me to the top of everybody's list. I suspect there are people who will take care of me lovingly if I need it, but they and other people in their world will still exist and deserve the focus of attention at some point.

What I want is that the growth I have achieved will be so deep that it will survive my growing old and continue to increase until the day I die.

I realize now that the concepts of maturity I have accepted are behind most of the resolves, the "I Wills" expressed in this book. While writing down what I will do, I am trying to grow into my age, learning in new situations to be "responsible, humble, objective, disciplined, empathetic, sociable and spiritual."

One of my perceived duties on the way is honest self-reflection for the purpose of correction and completion of unfinished work. Most of the unfinished work, I find, is me.

This morning I had a tiny dream, one of those fragmentary experiences when we are just falling asleep. Still tired after an uncomfortable night, sitting in my rocking chair, gazing into the woods, thinking my morning thoughts, my brain just went a little fuzzy. I had finished my coffee and put the cup down on the little stool beside me. I had been thinking about this unfinished essay on growing, searching for a little more understanding, when an image floated through my mind. I saw a woman moving toward me with a cup, holding it out to me. And I, sitting here in my chair, accepted the cup from her extended hand.

And then the vision was gone, and I knew I had slept for an instant. I had dreamed. And I realized, with some astonishment, that the woman who had walked toward me was also me. I remembered her clearly. She looked like the me in a certain old photograph, and she was wearing my robe. This is the first time, I believe, that I have seen myself in a dream. I did not know this could happen, and I perceived further that I had seen myself taking care of myself. There was something amiable and comfortable about the small scene, a picture of me living with myself, being responsible to myself, helpful to myself.

I find this an intriguing message from my subconscious mind. By extension it says interesting things.

I do think that genuine maturity, or my continued progress in that direction, is important first of all to me. I need to be happy with who am, because I live with myself and need to respect myself. I also need, for myself, to sense God's approval and to believe that my behavior serves my family and benefits others around me.

The existence of models is a wonderful thing when one wants to be more than she is. As a Christian I am supposed to say that Jesus is my model, and I do say it and mean it, though, looking at Jesus in this way, I can easily feel intimidated.

At the same time I am encouraged by an intriguing little story in the gospel of Luke about the twelve-year-old Jesus.

In a way typical of adolescents, Jesus wanted to be older than he was, and in an act thoughtless of his parents, he sneaked off to the temple to talk to the rabbis about theology when he was supposed to be with that big group of family and friends on the long hike back to Nazareth. It took Mary and Joseph three anxious and no doubt foot-sore days to go back and find him. In the conversation that ensued, they did not all understand one another perfectly, but Jesus went home with them and obeyed them and grew up.

He grew, Luke tells us, "in wisdom, in stature, and in favor with God and men."

There is a great deal of consolation in knowing that Jesus learned, grew, expanded into his character. He studied before arriving at his fierce opposition to legalism; he lived by the work of his hands to arrive at his profound sympathy for the poor; he got to know God and his purposes for him; and he developed relationships with people, becoming a leader and a healer. In the process of living, he became the man who at the age of thirty-three knew he was spiritually powerful, knew his own uniqueness and his greatness, and was aware of his unusual beginning and his impending death. Knowing all of this, he got up from the dinner table, wrapped a towel around his waist, knelt down and washed his disciples' weary feet. (John 13:3)

Though physically I seem to be changing in the opposite direction, I can still make progress in wisdom and in my relationship with God and the people around me. I think that being a Christian helps me in this whole process, because Christ's way is about growing us from the inside, not educating or manipulating us.

I suspect that growing happens while we are thinking of something else, maybe while we are trying merely to do what seems to be good. We don't notice progress until one day we take some old behavior out of the closet, try to put it on and discover that it doesn't fit anymore. We are bigger now. We can't act the way we used to act.

I Will Relinquish Control

I thought of my mother today. It was not a happy thought.

I had just opened my tax bill and discovered that it didn't even have my name on it.

Mother was ninety years old and in very poor health when my sister, her husband and I agreed that one of us needed the ability to access her bank account, the meager sum that came to her monthly and was spent mostly for medicines. She had suffered several illnesses during which she could barely sign a check to pay for things she needed from the store or the pharmacy.

My brother-in-law loved her and had so happily provided for her in his home. He called her "Mom" and was always gentle and considerate with her. Going into the little talk about money, we women let him take the lead, watched him kneel in front of her to be sure she heard, as he said that we wanted her to give at least one of us the right to sign checks on her account. He tried to explain this need to her without insinuating that she could become incapable or even die, leaving us unable to use her funds.

Her response was the last thing we expected. She burst into tears. She sobbed with her face in her hands, while we sat stunned and a little mystified. She could not explain why she cried except to say that it "upset" her.

The reason, of course, was that her checkbook was the last thing she had any control over. She had lost her car, her house, her neighbors, her church, her schedule, her responsibilities, her hearing, her ability to take a bath by herself. All she had left was a checkbook with a dab of money to pay for what she needed.

She cried. Then she agreed to sign the form. The incident left us all drained and sad.

Somehow this came back to me, because my property tax bill was puzzling. Not the amount. We pay a lot of tax for the privilege of living here, but we are used to it.

The name on my bill was the disturbing thing. My son's name, with the identification "successor trustee."

What did it mean? I got out last year's bill to compare. It bore my husband's name and mine, both of us identified as co-trustees. But Wayne had already passed away when that bill came. I had received a form from the assessor's office and, feeling insecure about how to respond to one question, I had taken the form to the office and filled it out in the presence of the assessor herself, so I knew it was accurate. Now this?

My name was totally gone from the tax bill. Our successor trustee was now responsible; that part was appropriate, I thought, except for the implication. They think I'm gone?!!

I also wondered if I would be wise to pay it, under my son's name. What would be the results down the road in case we should want to sell the house? There are tax exemptions for people selling their own home. But whose home is this under the law?

In the back of my mind was an unimaginable disaster that happened to a friend of mine several years ago. One month, with no warning at all, her social security check did not arrive. She made a call to ask questions and got puzzling answers. Another month and no check. And another. I am leaving out a lot of agony here to say that persistent protest finally unveiled the truth: Social Security Services thought she was deceased. Visits to the social security office with her card, her driver's license and her passport convinced no one that she was alive or who she claimed to be. She was helpless to manage her life. She didn't have money, nor could she use her credit cards or borrow from a bank, because her social security number was declared invalid.

She said, "Since I needed money, and people thought I was dead, I wondered if I could collect my life insurance."

Eventually, after months of frustration, Social Security Services discovered that a clerical error had led to the conclusion that this person with this number was deceased. They then sent two people to my friend's home and verified that she was who she said she was. She was alive and they now owed her considerable money.

With this horror story in my memory bank, I felt I had to appear at the tax office pronto and show them that I am still alive and ready to pay my taxes.

I talked with Dwight about it, and he agreed.

Long before all of this, Wayne and I had made numerous decisions reflecting the trust that existed in our family. When we moved to this little town and undertook the construction of a family home, we established a bank account with virtually everybody's name on it. Everybody was involved in building the house, so we imagined that any one of us who lived nearby might need access to the funds. The local bank was astonished that we were setting up an account with eight people empowered to take money from it.

We opened also our own joint account to receive and disperse our personal money, adding both Dwight and Sylvia as signees. Later I opened an account reserved for the operation of a small business I had, and I added Dwight as a signer to this account. In short, we have never tried to have anything that would be unavailable to our children.

About the time we finished the house and moved into it, we established a family trust and named our youngest son Dwight as successor trustee when both of us were either deceased or incapable. We also named our daughter Cynthia to take over in that capacity if Dwight should be unable.

A few years later when Wayne showed signs of poor health, we went to a local notary and signed a document saying that we were designating and appointing Dwight to serve as trustee because of this failing health. We signed a document, and life went along as always. Wayne got better and worse and better and we were always able to manage our affairs.

After his death I had some reason to go to the county Senior Center with a legal question. The lawyer asked to see our trust, read it and observed that we had appointed Dwight as trustee, but we needed another paper which Dwight would sign accepting the responsibility we had given him. Dwight then went to the office and signed, and this document was sent to the tax assessor.

Standing at the counter in the assessor's office, I learned that this had led to the assessor's recognition that Dwight is the responsible trustee for this property because I have "resigned." The polite gentleman who told me this also told me how to change it, if we wanted.

My first reaction was surprise, because I did not know I had resigned. This disturbed me for about five minutes, during which I walked back to my car. While putting the key into the ignition I realized that nothing I care about had changed. I live here in a house I can't take with me when I go. In the big scheme of things it is a borrowed house. My son has always been available to help me when I need help. I don't do much without consulting him. He has never inserted himself into my business when he was not needed. I trust him totally. No piece of paper governs our family relationships.

The situation, I realized, could not be better. When the responsibility is heavy, I have help available. When I can't manage he will step in, with the authority to do so. When I am tired I can quit. In fact, I have already resigned. What a relief!

I wrote Dwight an email explaining all of this. At the end of the letter I gloated that in our family we look at trusteeship as a headache somebody has to take on. In some families they look at it as control and advantage, because they don't fully trust one another.

He one-upped me, answering that it is not a headache but an honor and a privilege.

So easily my future has been secured. Bigger, younger, more capable hands are just under mine, ready either to help or to grab a responsibility and take care of it. If I stumble he will catch me.

I recognize that the need to be in control is stressful and tiring. It could even set me up to be suspicious of someone who wanted to help. Thinking that I don't have to be in control is positively liberating!

I hope my mother learned that in the short time she had left. I'm sorry it was so hard.

Leaving Home

Next to saying goodbye to loved people who die, abandoning home is the most wrenching experience I know.

Exploring the reasons for this, I have thought of so many things, relevant and irrelevant.

When this house was new and Vanessa, our youngest grandchild, was a baby and then a toddler and finally a little girl, she loved to sleep in our closet. During holidays, with adults in pairs filling all the bedrooms, and kids of various ages in sleeping bags around the pool table in the rec room, Grandma and Grandpa's walk-in closet was her choice.

On one side of the small room were Grandma's clothes. Dresses and coats and blouses and slacks hung from a rod; under them plastic tubs and shoe boxes filled all the space. On the opposite side were two chests of drawers; Grandpa's shirts and jackets and ties hung above these, and at the front end of the room on that side were Grandpa's suits and slacks. At the far end of the room a shelf supported by bricks held Grandpa's shoes, a random box or two, and an old movie projector that would show jumpy pictures of Vanessa's mother running off the end of a diving board before she knew that she couldn't swim.

In the middle of the closet was the walking space, Vanessa's chosen bedroom. With the walls and all of those soft things so close, she was protected. The dark was a cozy hiding place. With the door open, any squeak would bring somebody who was glad to see her anytime.

Children, like kittens and puppies, love small spaces. They will crawl into a box or a sack to play or sleep.

I figure that a house is an adult version of Grandma's closet. The world is too big and bewildering. The freedom of wide open spaces is exhilarating but leaves us vulnerable to dangers and discomforts. Without a tent we feel exposed. Knowing it is too flimsy to stop a bear, we are still able to fall asleep.

Without a house, man is a fox without a hole. A house is shelter, safety, privacy, ownership, event site, a door that can be shut, a treasure that can be shared. With the handle on the inside.

This is the loss of refugees and the homeless. It is practically everything.

But then, when empty, unneeded, a house is nothing but a possibility. It is only a shell until it takes the shape of the people who live there. It begins in a short time to reflect their values, needs, personalities, gifts.

This is what makes it so hard to leave a house long lived in—to sell it, rent it, vacate it, reject it for another. It is not just the house we leave; it is the life we lived there, the effort we made to get it the way it is, the events that happened in the rooms, the memories that hover in the spaces, the pain we endured here. That's what we think when we go—that we are leaving all of this, abandoning a friend who stood with us through it all.

When I said I would carry on and meant that I would stay in my house, leaving seemed like betrayal, like the rejection of a gift, ignoring a sacrifice, not honoring the place where sacred events took place, forgetting what was planned with me in mind, running away from the bathtub in which Wayne died.

This was not my home, but ours. He would have stayed, I think, to die in the place where I died. He would stay to die in the place he made, because he was a builder. He treasured the past, kept a record always. In so many ways, he never wandered far from his roots.

But a builder of houses knows what a house is. And what a house isn't.

Contractors build houses. They call them homes to sell them, because a home is a warm, welcoming place, worth so much more money than a house.

A house is just a house until somebody lives in it and makes it home, and then, when the people leave, it becomes just a house again. Oddly, I have left ten or twelve of them without regret (not to mention one with my heart in shreds). When I saw them again, they were just houses. New owners had made them forget us.

That doesn't make it easier to leave this house built with the hands of my family. They came from near and far to build it for this one reason: at last their parents would be home from wandering the earth and loving other people in other places. They meant to keep us here. We meant to stay.

Leaving will feel like abandoning a lover, a house that became more than a house. I shall be jealous of someone else.

They are brave people, my sons and daughters; they have given me permission to go.

I Will Take the Initiative

Families need to talk. About a lot of things. The future of those who are aging is one.

I have decided that initiating the conversation about getting old is the responsibility of the one who is aging. She knows what she has lost. No one notices it more than she does. In fact no one else knows how often she forgets the word she needs; she covers it up in conversation, finding another word, talking around it. No one else knows how often she pees in her pants on the way to the bathroom. No one else feels the pain in her back when she stands at the sink washing dishes.

Or, suppose they do know. Maybe they have noticed things, things Mom has not admitted. This is hard for the younger generation. They are reluctant to sit down with an aging parent and say, "Look, I'm worried about your being here alone." This feels like a role reversal.

This is why I opened a conversation with my family. I didn't start by saying, "I can't do this much longer."

I don't even know that; maybe I can do it a lot longer. Or maybe some sudden catastrophe will change everything. What I know is that when the time comes I may have a few problems. We need to talk about my options. I need help to discover them.

And there are places I don't want to be. If I move I want to choose where I am going. That means I have to do it while my children know that I am making rational decisions. And if I am going anywhere, there is about a year of work needed to get ready, which means two years because I am not ready to stop all the fun, the satisfying things I do while dismantling this big house and throwing away my accumulated precious trash.

And the big house happens to belong to all of us. It is my home and my children's inheritance. In my mind I am a caretaker, saving it for them, making sure they get it in good condition. But since they all now have homes of their own, the question is imminent: what happens to this house when I am gone?

The answer to this question changes what I should do to get ready. Should I, for instance, leave the lovely hanging lights made in Hebron and Damascus? Yes, if one of my children will be living in this house; no, if it will go to a stranger.

And, in any case, what happens to that nearly immovable pool table in the rec room?

So this question, so crucial for me, is really for them. They have to decide. I have to give them time. They have to understand that I don't have forever.

And I read in a book, by an expert in the field of aging and what we do about it, that the reason so many elderly people are unhappy in the places where they live is that they did not choose these places. Their children chose.

What do the children want? For Mom to be in a place where they don't have to worry. She will be safe. She will be fed. She will take her medicine. If she falls, someone will be there to do the appropriate thing.

But what does Mom want? Space for her favorite books, people who share her interests, good strong wifi, too (she still communicates!), a familiar kind of worship service, visits from her grandchildren. Some privacy, too, some dignity. And a reason for being in the world. I can leave behind my nice oak bed, but I have to take with me or find there the causes that drive me, stimulation—intellectual and artistic—to produce and grow, reasons to get out of bed in the morning. If these things are not present in that place, I will not be safe there.

I want to choose.

So, I wrote a letter to my family, raising my questions. There was no immediate result.

I started doing research. I went to an independent living center and asked for a tour. I saw the atmosphere, noticed the size of apartments, talked about prices, picked up the week's menus, came home with contact information. I went to another state, asked my daughter to take me to places in the community. In my mind I compared places, prices, problems, possibilities.

Later I learned that one of my grandsons was upset about this. "How could you even think of putting Grandma in one of those places?"

I promised myself to have a talk with him about that. Maybe he misunderstands "those places." I want him to know that I am choosing, and I am not afraid. But I appreciate his concern. I want him to know that when we get to any new stage of life, we can get there ready, the way he graduated from college ready to get a job and start paying his own bills.

There are so many reasons, emotional and practical, that we have to think about this big subject together. Some of the reasons happen to be painful.

Leaving this house will be a gut-wrenching experience. I admit this.

Going to a new place will be an adventure. I will make it so.

And looking at another of these possibilities this very week, I realized that all of those places will limit me in the end. Preparing my meals for me will make me first glad and then sorry that I can't do it anymore. Putting me in a small apartment will cause me to walk a lot less than I do in this big house. Since there is an elevator, I may get lazy and ignore the stairs. If I sit in my chair longer than usual today, I find I don't even want to get up. I know the next step is being unable to get up.

Here I have the big outdoors, a forested lot that belongs to me, and the street with its friendly neighbors and a few not-too-friendly dogs. I have noticed that it is not just walking that invigorates me; the fresh air has a role.

I am picky; I want a lot of things.

A friend advises me to go while I am still coping and enjoying life here. I can see why she is right. At the same time I can see that I don't want to go precisely because I am coping and enjoying life here. It is a puzzle.

My family came through. They met through their computer screens and discussed honestly and amicably my needs, their hopes, the blunt facts, and a few unknowns. The result is that I am free to do what I want, when I want, and they are prepared to give me organized help. They made action plans; we all have something to do.

When I get to some new place, I will need more than the things I have put in my suitcases. I will need everything I know about how to live and probably some things that other people know. That's why the decisions had to come out of conversation. And why I took the initiative.

But don't worry. I mean to do it thoughtfully, methodically, logically (which could be a euphemism for dragging my feet).

I Will Have a Bad Day

Sometimes I think I am doing really well.

Look, I say to myself. I am 89. Living alone, shopping, making meals, keeping house, inviting guests.

I lead a Bible study on Wednesday mornings. I take a turn once a month working with children in Sunday School. I go to council meetings and make reports.

I accept a speaking engagement once in a while and sell a few books.

I drive wherever I need to go, over twisty mountain roads and down to the city. Even at night, I come home alone to the empty house.

I pay my bills on time, keep accounts, comparing expenditures with the budget I wrote.

This summer I got my house repaired, painted and de-pested. Yay!

I still write a little bit. It is harder than it used to be, but I do it, because I haven't run out of things to say.

On hot afternoons I go down to my cool basement and work in my messy library, separating books into piles and bags and shelves, designated for my church, my local library, particular members of my family and the recycle bin. (I have noticed in this process, that books, like people, get old. They get brittle and hard to read. They get separated from their context.)

What am I saying? I survive and keep plugging. That's the point I'm making. I think I am smart and brave and healthy and resourceful.

And then I have a day like yesterday.

I got up with a schedule in mind, having determined somehow that I must leave home at 9:50 A.M. I would see my GP, then get my annual hearing test. I would go to a store and buy some frozen cod. (I have not been eating enough fish). Then I could go home and have a sandwich or maybe eat lunch out. Thinking about this, I had another thought. Since I would be in the right vicinity I could use the opportunity to find the waste disposal place and finally get rid of these little bottles of ink and Wayne's collection of old medicines. I had gotten up early and time was not an issue until I realized that I probably should empty all the pill bottles and take the pills in a plastic bag. Emptying bottles was easy but prying a jillion pills out of their one-by-one spaces in aluminized sheets was tedious and time-consuming. So, on the verge of being late for my medical appointment, I had to rush. Two minutes down the road I realized I had left my hearing aids and had to come back for them.

At Dr. Young's office, the secretary was confused by my arrival, half an hour late. My appointment was for 10:00, not 10:30. She was right; that's what was written in my little agenda, which I had not looked at since yesterday. If I waited long enough, maybe the doctor could still see me, she said. But if I waited too long I would miss the hearing test, so I rescheduled and went to Miracle Ear, where the secretary said she had written me in for August 31, not August 3. (I was convinced that was her error not mine, but there was no slot for me today.)

Finding the dump was not easy, even with the help of my GPS, but I found it, sat in a slow moving line of vehicles for half an hour, trying to think positive thoughts. I left my hazardous waste, went back to town, joined the queue at the pharmacy drive-through to pick up a prescription, which was not ready, had a Chinese lunch, put half my food in a take-home box and forgot and left it on the table, went back to the pharmacy for my meds, ready at last, then found a cleaners and left my comforter, in exchange for a yellow receipt that says I can reclaim it for thirty-eight dollars. At that point I decided that I was too tired to go to the store for cod and drove home, weary and downhearted about my mistakes. Along the road I began to dread opening the door of this empty house.

It happens like this. Not often, but it happens. I make mental mistakes. I think things through but not all the way. I suspect I am becoming old and inept. I need my friend, the other half of the two of us, the half that would have said at 9:15, "But, Loves, your appointment is at 10:00, isn't it?" The one who would have gone with me and would have known how to get to the dump, and probably would have noticed my box of food on the restaurant table and picked it up. The one who would, otherwise, be waiting here to listen to my story and say, "Bummer, Sweetie. Sit down here; let me get you a cool drink."

Most days I am energetic. Some days I am even efficient. Now and then I am old and clumsy, and tired and discouraged.

Swallowing this dose of realism, I get in bed, say a one-sentence prayer that tomorrow will be better and turn out the light.

I tell myself, You just had a bad day; get over it.

I Will Face the Truth

Promises are easy. Vows, from one who is young, about what she will do when she is old are hardly worth listening to. They seem important, but it turns out that they are like vows to walk out of quicksand, from someone who never experienced quicksand.

And it could be that seventy-five is young; eighty and eighty-five, too, probably are young, compared to ninety. Maybe I was a bit more perceptive yesterday than today.

In his marvelous, thought-provoking book, *Being Mortal*, Atul Gawande tells us about "quicksand." (My word choice not his) Bones lose density, arteries harden, muscles thin, bowels slow down, glands stop functioning, and brains shrink. There is little any of us can do to slow the process; there is nothing we can do to stop it.

These are the facts, straight from a caring doctor.

"By age eighty-five," the doctor says, "working memory and judgment are sufficiently impaired that 40 percent of us have textbook dementia."

215

". . . the amount of light reaching the retina of a healthy sixty-year-old is one-third that of a twenty-year-old."

"The risk of a fatal car crash with a driver who's eighty-five or older is three times higher than it is with a teenage driver. The very old are the highest-risk drivers on the road."

Just a few of his stunning declarations.

This is hard to read when one is eighty-nine, alone in a big house, writing brave intentions for her descendants, mopping the kitchen floor, driving herself wherever she needs to go, teaching a Bible study every Wednesday, trying to keep on becoming a responsible adult.

That's me.

Ordinarily I keep my anxieties under control. I have lived a lot in fearful situations without falling apart, in the process learning what I can endure and what I should not ask myself to endure. I go to bed alone in a big house and go to sleep (unless I drank that ill-advised cup of coffee in the afternoon). I don't spend a lot of time thinking "what-if." I usually don't get scared of things not yet proven to be real.

I once had twenty rules for surviving civil war. One of them was, "Turn back if you come to a small hand-written sign that says, 'Beware of sniper.'"

Good rule. Helped me keep safe.

Then lately, I read Gawande's book, and I got the message that I am flying into the teeth of a tsunami and there is no steering wheel in this vehicle.

I admit the truth, I am a little bit afraid now. Brittle bones, weak muscles, hard arteries, slow bowels, these could be minor things, nuisances I could contend with (I think). Loss of vision is a harder thing, something I don't really want to contemplate. It is so important to be able to read when one has not learned well how to listen.

But my brain! I need my brain! I don't want to get lost on the way home from book club meeting. I don't want to forget the names of my friends. I don't want to know I have dementia. But especially, I don't want other people to know it when I don't. (Pride survives almost everything.)

A couple of years ago I had a transient, recurring pain in one exact spot in my head, so my GP ordered a scan. Nothing interesting showed up. A sideline of the boring result was "brain shrinkage normal for age." At the time I thought that was a passable report when actually it was terrible news! No one had explained to me that dementia is normal for my age!

It's not that I want to be sharper than the average person who has stepped into the quicksand, but I've just realized that the problems and purposes of being eighty-nine really need a sixty year-old brain. This is something that slipped my attention when I was sixty. I might have started my old-age ruminations sooner.

So, will there be a sign telling me to turn back?

And what does this do to all my vows? I have vowed so many things: to accept new-fangled inventions, to throw away my trash (things I love that nobody else wants), to invite people for lunch, to live for some serious purposes, to wear my hearing aids and visit my dentist and play dress-up and pour out blessings on my grandchildren. I have even promised to write timely essays full of wisdom, and dance at everybody's wedding, all the while admitting that I need help learning to use this new Word program or changing the light bulb over my mirror.

So what can I say now about my promises? "Everybody, please take them with a grain of salt?" (Imagine! Marketing this book with very big salt shaker.)

The serious point I am coming to here is that all my vows are totally sincere. I intend to keep every one of them . . . up to the very day when I can't. I have to acknowledge that the day will come. My promises, it seems, have expiration dates, but I don't exactly know what they are. Some will run out before others.

I hope my family, my friends, even everyone who reads my vows, will interpret them to mean that I at least know what I want to do. I want to do what my family needs me to do, things that use my gifts and enrich my days, whatever I know is right. So, that I intend to do.

Giving up is not one of the things I promised. I won't add it now, because I honestly don't have any talent for giving up or very much experience. However, I have learned how to face facts and submit to the truth. I will do that.

Probably.

When a cop takes my driver's license, when I can't make myself a bowl of soup, when I get lost between home and the grocery, I will admit it. Maybe not the first time it happens. But about the third time I probably will have to say it.

I will adjust to the new facts. This may be the hardest of my vows to keep. You may remind me that I wrote it down.

I promise to face the truth. If I am not ready when the end of my independence is in sight, I will get ready. If there is time. If I am capable. If someone who loves me delivers the news.

I Will Choose, Again

Subtle changes are happening in my daily life:

I notice that my to-do list is too long. Again. Still.

I hesitate before accepting responsibilities.

I get along with a shorter variety of foods.

I am happy for someone else to make dinner.

I miss scheduled meetings, make more trips to the doctor, fall asleep with a book in my hand.

I value more days with no reason to leave the house.

These are facts I acknowledge with regret, recognizing the narrowing that takes place in the lives of the elderly. Some things that I chose to do in the past now fail to excite me.

The problem begins with good, happy things.

I have so many people in my life: the Fuller clan, one sister yet, my little church family, my neighbors, my high school classmates, an old roommate, people on the other side of the world, some with whom I endured a civil war, others with whom I shared a three-day conference and bonded for life.

I enjoy so many books: novels, essays, memoirs, short stories, poetry, my fraying Bible.

I love such a variety of music: Beethoven and Bernstein, the Hallelujah Chorus and Amazing Grace, orchestras and saxophones, pianos and guitars, the waltz and the jitterbug, choirs and Elvis, and Peter, Paul and Mary.

I am fascinated by sports: baseball and basketball and marathons.

The truth is that I still care about a great many causes: personal, moral, political, religious. I have been a crusader for world peace, a sympathizer of the Palestinians, a giver to refugees. I invested a big piece of my life in the creation of Christian literature in the Arabic language. I have wanted everyone to have health insurance as good as mine and stood up for the right of every child to be born because she is wanted. I ponder how to make sense of my life story, what I learned, where I failed, relating it all to my time in history, if I can. I keep searching, trying to understand how we got our world into such a mess, wanting to see God's hand in what has happened, God's heart in it all. At the same time I aspire to wash the car and know trivia, and I keep trying to expand my vocabulary.

Clearly I am falling behind in some of these projects.

What I am saying is that over the course of a long life, the time comes to simplify. Last year I had to be choosy. This year a little more so. Limited stamina, less spring in my legs, less ability to multitask, poorer eyesight, less capacity in a shrinking brain: these are things I can abhor and push against, but not things I can ignore.

That's why I have come to this necessity again, the need to choose.

Choosing is simply a way of ranking issues according to importance to me and my world and now especially according to practicality. Is it first or middle or last? Is it doable for me or not?

I must take care of things I care about the most.

I must not accept responsibilities and then not deliver.

I must consider the best use of my own gifts. And time. Especially my time.

Not wanting to leave all of this to chance and go to bed discouraged or wake up surprised that I left the dishes in the sink, failed to pay my bills and neglected someone who loves me, I will have to make many choices.

Which news stories I listen to, which books I read, which meetings I attend, what music haunts my day, the Google search I begin, the responsibility I accept, the calls I return, the causes I support, the tasks I can mark off the list and whether I walk today or sit here.

First of all, I feel I must pray for wisdom. It is too late for bad decisions.

I have been through all of this before. I have made choices. Now there is something else. It is not just activities I must choose. I need to choose an attitude.

What shall I say to myself when I subtract something from my life? When I give up an unfinished dream? When I save my strength in one place to use it in another? Shall I be angry? or disappointed? or sad? or relieved? Shall I regret or celebrate this new stage of life?

Can I accept that there is a time for everything, a time to do it all, and a time to trust most of it to another generation?

I think I have arrived at the front edge of a new stage of life, like the others raising questions, maybe the same questions, requiring now a new kind of courage and some different answers.

Traveling by Remembering

My son Tim asked me if there was any place I would like to go, the implication being that I don't have a lot of time, and a little more travel might be on my bucket list.

Tim is a traveler. And a hiker and a climber. When he doesn't answer his phone on a Saturday I immediately picture him on some Washington mountainside. If he doesn't return the call for three days, I start guessing: Spain? Switzerland?

But he is also a dutiful son, willing to take his eighty-nine-year-old mother wherever she would like to go. At first, I said I didn't want to go anywhere.

He said, "Isn't there someplace that you and Dad talked about going?"

I finally admitted that we had done some dreaming about a train trip across Canada. Hearing nice things about the beauty of our neighbor to the north, we imagined seeing it slow and easy from the windows of a train, eating in the dining car, maybe getting off someplace late in the day, sleeping in a bed, and waiting for the next train going our way. (Why let Canada roll past the windows in the dark?) We dreamed; that's all. There were so many other things to do with our money. And we had traveled. The day we said that yes to the opportunity to go and live in the Arab world, we unwittingly became travelers. Thirty-odd years later, when we built this house, we were travel weary, needing a home.

Tim and I have not yet been to Canada, either. We have not even studied train schedules. It's amazing how life gets in its own way. But that's O.K.

I have discovered that my memories are a cheap, convenient way to travel.

In Lebanon we lived for several years on the side of a hill, facing a little canyon. On the other side of the canyon the mountain lifted up forests and villages and roads and colors and changing moods. The sun came up from behind that mountain and, in evening, the moon. Late in the day, not always but often, there was a lovely few minutes, as the day faded and night was still a mere suspicion, when all the hills were lavender, the pale, gentle sister of purple, everything in sight lavender, like a beautiful girl in her evening gown. I used to stand on my balcony and wait for it and try to memorize it, for the time when I would not see it anymore.

Once Tim came back from the U.S., arriving home at this fragile, favorite moment and exclaimed, "Ohhh, I have forgotten that Lebanon is this color!" as though it were not a fickle and fragile hue, going away even as it came. So far as I know, no other place in the world is that color ever, and even the memory is a delicate thing, like a dream not understood.

Beirut had a lot of overpasses. Without them we may never have managed to drive across some of those congested roads. There was nothing else remarkable about these urban bridges; they rose up a bit and sloped down again, without engaging our minds. Except for one. On the northern edge of the city, toward Jounieh, maybe around Antelias, there was a bridge notable for the traffic sign warning drivers of its limitations. Simple, matter-of–fact, non-verbal, the sign reminded us of the unpleasant situation, at the same time, provoking a smile. It was a picture of a tank with a slash through it.

Preparing to come home to California for a year, we realized that San Francisco and Beirut are exactly opposite one another on the globe at the same parallel. And Pan Am promoted a round-the-world ticket that was good for a year, an intriguing option for going home and back. The only reason that west to east was two hundred dollars per person cheaper was that it was the more popular route. So just once we paid the difference, for all seven of us, and came home across the East. There were several tantalizing places to stop and look around. Afghanistan, for instance, where I wanted to go simply because I had read an interesting book about it. Though it was a little out of the way, Afghanistan was accessible from Tehran where we had already spent a tiresome month, after being taken out of Amman on a military cargo plane just after the June 1967 Arab-Israeli war.

So we deviated from the regular route across the Far East and took a side trip to Kabul.

For reasons probably unknown to us, even at the time, our family was sent out of the transit lounge in Tehran to stand with our luggage, quite a long time, in the shelter of the building. We were awaiting a signal to walk out to a plane that was sitting on the tarmac.

It was in the hour just before sunup, a little bit cold, and, as the light grew, we could see big thunderheads in the east. These great piles of clouds, in changing shapes, growing bright on the edges, seemed to be holding back the sunrise. And suddenly a golden beam burst through a hole, like a spotlight tilted upward, and as it faded, another in a different place, and another, and in this uncertain, stuttering fashion, the sun rose, appearing here, then there, disappearing, then exploding through breaks in the clouds, sending long sharp-edged blades of light in one direction then another, each a surprise. And finally, the whole blazing fire, at which one dare not stare, mounted the sky. In my mind there was music, the accompaniment this show deserved. I seemed to hear the cry of a bugle, the pounding of a drum, a quiver of strings, the full orchestra surge.

This is, without exception, the most amazing sunrise I have ever witnessed. With the memory I always get a line from Kipling about the sun coming up like thunder. Until then I had always wondered what Kipling meant.

If I talk about places I have traveled, I just have to tell you that one day we rented a jeep and drove all day in the mountains outside of Kabul with only a vague idea of where we were going. The terrain was brown and bare, the road rough and sometimes steep. As we came into a small village we saw and smelled a bakery, just at the side of the road. With skillful hands a man was shaping these great pieces of dough into a large, unusual shape, long, and bigger at one end than the other. With some kind of tool he punched the dough in multiple places, brushed it with oil, then picked it up on a long-handled wooden shovel and slid it into an open oven, full of flames. What came out looked like a snowshoe and was the best bread we had ever eaten, yeasty and nutty and satisfyingly genuine. We sat at a little table outside with small cups of coffee and ate these wholesome hot loaves as they came out of the oven, feeling privileged, and telling each other that most of the people in the world had no idea what bread was supposed to be, because they had never been here in this rural village on a mountainside in Afghanistan.

A local teen-ager came and sat by our Tim. Over and over, with some difficulty each time, he said, "I want to be your friend." This seemed to be the only sentence he could say in English, and Tim who was 13, red-haired and getting a sunburn, did not know how to answer this impossible request.

I wonder now: Did it happen here or the previous summer in Tehran? But in Tehran we were living in a luxury hotel, and the setting probably would have been a swimming pool, so I think it was Afghanistan. Truthfully, anywhere in the Middle East, a young man wanted an American friend. Over and over we discovered that, making doubly sad the things that happened later.

By the time a year had passed after our visit, no one would think of going to Afghanistan to wander around.

Once, walking on the street in Cairo, I suddenly stopped to avoid stepping into a picture that was about to be snapped. On one side of the sidewalk a group of boys in short-pants uniforms, like scouts, posed proudly, stiffly, with serious faces. And on the opposite side of the walk, a man with a camera in front of his face was counting.

When the boys, young adolescents, saw me backing out of their picture, spontaneous smiles broke out on their faces. One of them shouted, "Come!" speaking English, motioning with his hand, in a Middle Eastern way, his palm turned down, his fingers raking me toward him. And others joined him in Arabic calling, "Yes, yes, come. Get in the picture."

No way! Why?

I resisted, and they insisted. The photographer said, "Of course. They want you."

Not finding a graceful way to refuse, I stood on the end of a row, to one side.

"No, no, here," they said and parted to open a space for me.

When it was done, I left quickly, but turned to wave, and they all waved at me, saying, "Shukran, shukran." I don't know why, but Middle Easterners always say thank you after you pose for a picture with them.

Thirty years later the memory makes me smile. And I wonder still what their mothers and fathers said when they got these snapshots of their sons' outing with the scouts, and right in the middle of one picture there was this strange woman, blond and foreign, and the boys all looking so pleased with themselves.

Considering how much I have forgotten, it is surprising that I still remember a black and white picture in a fifth-grade textbook. The words underneath said, "the bazaar in Baghdad." I learned that strange word: bazaar. And that pleasant name: Baghdad. Two famous rivers, the Tigris and the Euphrates, were a part of this place. Sitting at my desk in that simple school room in 1939, I experienced an unexplainable longing. The wish to see that place was a secret I didn't even know how to tell.

Many years later I sent books from Beirut to Baghdad. A priest who came out to Amman had seen in a bookstore there *Taraneem al-Iman* (Hymns of Faith), a book my staff and I had labored over for four long years. In it we preserved Arabic translations of a hundred great hymns, passed to them by churches in the West, and a wealth of Arabic songs, spontaneous creations out of little churches in Egypt, Jordan and Lebanon, written down and shared for the first time.

This was during the period of sanctions against Hussein, and the priest wanted a thousand books, apologizing for begging, because he could send no money out of Iraq. I made phone calls and found money to cover the costs. The Lebanese Bible Society was willing to put them on a truck with Bibles, and I sent the priest a thousand hymnbooks to share around in his city, the last of the 17,000 I had printed only a year before.

Years later in my home in California I received a phone call from Iraq. The young Lebanese man who had designed that hymnbook was now a translator for the American Army. He wanted to tell me a story.

Sitting at his desk, working with a pile of papers, he heard humming. The cleaning woman, clad in black, was singing under her breath a tune he recognized, and he began to hum along quietly. Suddenly he stopped, realizing this was a song from our book, Taraneem al-Iman. He had to ask, "Where did you get this song?"

She went into the little closet where she slept and brought out five pages, stapled together, with hymns photocopied on both sides. "This is very valuable," she said, "because no one can buy this book anymore. I have only these. My favorites. One of the believers gave them to me when I became a follower of Jesus, because I love them so much."

Lately I discovered in my files a letter from a pastor, thanking me for the portion his church had received from those 1000 books. I treasure the story and that letter more than a ticket to Baghdad.

I bought an elephant in Africa.

I could have had a giraffe. I loved the giraffes in Kenya, with their tattooed fur, the surprising grace they achieved with front legs longer than the back and such small heads so far from their shoulders. But I thought I would always be afraid that the spindly neck would break. An elephant is so solid and sturdy.

Choosing mine was difficult. She had to fit in my suitcase, without pushing it over the airline weight limit.

If I knew, I would say what kind of wood she is carved from, but either I forgot to ask or have forgotten the answer. She is dark brown except for her ample haunches and tail that are lighter, along with the edge of her left ear and the left side of her trunk. She stands almost ten inches high. Her baby, walking beside her right foot is nearly four inches, a little higher than her knee. An attentive mother, she touches her infant with a curled trunk. This is what endeared her to me.

If her white tusks are not ivory, you can't prove it by me, and they appear to be weapons guarding her baby.

Our friends Betty and Harold, who spoke Swahili, made the deal for me with the carver whose stand we happened to see beside the road. I paid seventeen American dollars for this work of art.

Less than an hour later we stopped at a big warehouse where Harold hoped to buy corn meal. There was a famine in Kenya, and he was responsible for supplying this staple food to a certain Christian community. But we found the warehouse empty. While he stood discussing the situation with the manager, and Wayne stood staring, incredulous, into the cavernous emptiness of the building, I sat in the car with Betty, waiting. Among the people who walked up and down the dusty street, there came a girl who recognized the car, and Betty. The two of them talked through the open window and, of course, I understood nothing.

The girl moved away to stand in the shade of the building, emotionless in her colorful, flour-sack kind of cotton dress, and Betty explained. She had requested money, enough to pay for her final year of high school. Actually, it was the fee for two years, because last year she had not had money to pay, and now the administrator had told her she had to bring the money for two years, or they could not admit her.

"She is a smart girl," Betty told me, "and she wants so much to go to school, but they are really poor. Their house burned recently and right now her brother is in the hospital. When he is released soon, they have to pay for his care. There is no way they can send her to school."

The girl stood leaning against a wall, staring at nothing, a grim sort of patience on her round face, but something else that I thought was a fearful hope. She had presented her case to the American who was surely rich.

"Of course, I can't give her the money. I would have a thousand kids on my doorstep tomorrow morning," Betty said.

I said, "How much money are we talking about?"

And she said, "Seventeen dollars."

Seventeen dollars! Rarely had I been so pricked in my conscience.

I said, "Could I give it to her?"

"Only if we make it very plain that it comes from you, not me."

We called the girl into the car to sit beside me in the back seat, and Betty told her. I almost understood when she said, "The tourist lady wants to help you."

A mere hint of happiness flickered across the girl's placid face and was gone.

"I know your family has many needs," Betty told her. "You must make it plain. The money is for school, nothing else."

I had American bills rolled up in my fist, a ten and seven ones. She barely opened her limp hand. Her lips quivered ever so slightly. She sat staring at the money.

"Tell your parents," Betty said, "It was the American tourist lady who gave it to you. For school, nothing else."

The men came and we drove away, not knowing when there would be corn meal. Harold was worried that his people were hungry.

The elephant traveled well from Kenya to Lebanon with me and then to California. She still walks with her baby on my entry table for part of every year. Once she went to church with me to help me talk about Africa.

Sometimes she sits in a closet, waiting. I have willed her to one of my grandsons, along with this story.

I Will Celebrate

Before that final game in the league playoffs, the basketball coach had invited us to a celebration, the celebration that would happen if the American Community School won. And they won.

Wayne and I didn't even have a kid on the team. Our sons were gymnasts and wrestlers, but Wayne was always doing something for the athletic department, and I guess the basketball team had profited, so there we were.

This was in Beirut. I don't remember who the unfortunate loser was that night. It could have been any American high school from Jedda to Katmandu. Traveling to compete was a big deal, requiring visas, health certificates and big money.

What I remember is a rather small room, maybe a faculty break room with a small refrigerator and a coffee pot in a corner, a table, fifteen or twenty chairs, athletic slogans on the walls. The table had become the focus of the room, bearing platters of food, which I honestly don't remember, but I would be surprised if it didn't include flat Lebanese bread with multiple small dishes of hummus, olives and salty pickles, the little meat pies we Americans liked to call "Lebanese pizza" and a big traditional version with pepperoni from the Popeye's down on the Corniche. The coach was still in the locker room with the team, and the handful of people who had arrived picked up food and drinks and sat down with paper plates on their knees and cups in their hands, and in the process found that we were all strangers.

Suddenly a man burst through the door and stopped abruptly to look around, as though suspecting he was in the wrong place. He said, "What is this? A wake? I thought we won; I thought we were celebrating."

Which raises a question . . .

Recently I looked for a definition of the word "celebrate." Then I wondered if something was wrong with my dictionary. The synonyms for celebrate are: perform, solemnize, honor, mark, observe and finally one called an "informal" definition: "to have a convivial good time."

That last one is what that little group of American strangers in Beirut was not doing, until a genuine partier bounced in and accused us of acting like losers.

Maybe the best celebrations happen spontaneously. When delirious winners tear down the goalpost. When a long, hard job is complete. When something precious that was lost is found. A ceasefire is announced. Bombs stop falling. A soldier comes home. The cancer is in remission. We throw up our hands and shout and sing and cry and dance a jig and high-five one another. We say, Thank you, Lord, and collapse and let the tension drain out of our limbs. That's celebrating.

But, of course my Webster's is right. A celebration is first of all a pause to recognize the importance of an achievement, to notice a milestone or the end of a road, to give us time to think and declare that something significant has happened, something that gives us satisfaction, or frees us from an obligation, or closes a door.

In the spring of 1975 civil war had broken out in Lebanon and life was so dangerous that schools were dismissed, administrators casually handing out diplomas to graduates, without any program or festivity. Years later I was sitting with a young man who finished high school that year, and he told me that occasionally he had the heart-stopping feeling that he never graduated and had to go to his files and find the diploma to be sure.

Even a less than happy event may need a marker, a formal observance that enables us to put something behind us and start over. I know a woman who divorced her husband after twenty-five years and insisted on a ceremony. It was a solemn occasion, attended by close friends. In a brief program the two people admitted their good intentions, failures and regrets. They made promises about what they would and would never do to one another in the future. They signed statements. They drank toasts to one another, before saying goodbye.

I think I missed some great opportunities to celebrate, especially in my work in Lebanon. When a new book came off the press, I usually just turned my attention to other materials in the proofreading stage, to some being prepared for publication by editors, to work under translation, and covers being designed, to manuscripts being considered, to books still being written. All these stages happened simultaneously in a publishing house. Taking time to celebrate might have helped me realize that I was doing well or not.

Sometimes I have been sorry later that I did not take time to celebrate, but I have always been glad when I did.

On the landscape of our lives there are events and experiences that are like mountain peaks. Our memory can always find them. Planting our flag on top, that's a celebration.

My friend Joan, just before her eightieth birthday, announced that she wanted to celebrate by walking across the Golden Gate Bridge. Since she would need a bit of help, at least a ride to the bridge and back home again, she talked with her family about this hope. They loved the idea and one by one announced a wish to go with her.

In the end it was a family event, three generations walking together, one eighty year-old, several adults in their fifties, college kids and teenagers, children and a babe in arms. It was a cold day, and high in the air in the middle of the strait, the Bay in one direction, the Pacific in the other, seagulls flying, there is always a stiff wind, so they were bundled in coats and scarves and kept a brisk pace.

Of course, they paused at times, to stand at the rail and look down on a ship gliding out to sea, to note the size of the twisted cables holding up this wonder of a bridge, to feel the sway of its improbable movement in the wind, and admire its pillars, orange against the blue of space.

Joan herself stopped in the middle of the bridge. Ignoring the wind, she looked back over the route she had just come and thought about her past and the route of her life, then she turned around and, facing the city of San Francisco, thought about what she hoped for the future.

Now Joan is approaching her ninetieth birthday. For the past year she has been reading *Astrophysics for People in a Hurry*, and has been fascinated with the stars. This led to a decision about what to do for her next celebration. She has told the family that she wants to visit the planetarium in Golden Gate Park, so of course the whole family is getting excited about seeing the stars with Grandma Joan.

When Wayne and I turned eighty, we decided to throw ourselves a party. We could do that easily—have a party together, because he was only forty-five days older than I. Getting our big family all together in one room at the same time requires considerable communication and compromising. We finally chose the date when the most people could be present, and we celebrated for two days.

Several people came early to help us shop, prepare food and decorate the house. We meant to have both solemn recognition and plenty of conviviality.

The first day was for friends as well as family, and we had a grand open house with a specific afternoon hour set for a program. While most of our guests were local, several came from distances up to five hundred miles, and we prepared the way for these, securing hotel rooms nearby, but a few people astonished us by appearing at the door, like apparitions out the past. Part of the program we designed to help our friends know better our children and grandchildren, our children introducing their own children and one another.

The second day was a family-only event. With everyone gathered in the living room, Wayne and I reminisced, telling stories about this special group of people, things the others could know only from us, especially sharing with our grandchildren stories about their parents when they were young.

Only from us could they know that their brilliant Uncle Tim announced when he was three years old that he was the stupidest person in the world, because we had a huge bookcase full of books and he could not read even one of them.

They needed us to tell them about Jan's courage at three, singing through days of darkness and painful injections, her eyes bandaged, her arms in splints after eye surgery, never crying once, having been told that tears would spoil the doctor's work.

We thought they should know who lost his diaper and ran up the street naked, who talked back as soon as she could say words, who really wanted to be a bird, who was a little monster at four in afternoon but turned magically into an angel at sight of a graham cracker with peanut butter.

And we gave gifts, presenting meaningful objects from our own possessions to each of our children. For instance, we gave Cynthia a small cedar chest that says "Mother" on the lid and belonged to Grandmother Anderson, having been a gift from her daughter who saved it for me after Grandmother's death. Inside the chest were several fascinating and useless items, such as a letter I wrote to Grandmother when I was six.

To some we gave small treasures picked up through our long lives, sometimes as gifts to us, sometimes found in strange places, all with stories behind them.

When Wayne was dying we planned a party, not in spite of his dying, but because of it. It was Memorial Day 2017, and our son Tim was determined to honor his dad with a piano concert.

More than fifty people filled our house and spilled onto the deck. The rented baby grand stood in our living room. Folding chairs filled every space, enabling everyone to sit and listen, and many could see the pianist as well. In his big recliner near the piano, Wayne was positioned so that he could see the hands on the keyboard.

Before he played, Tim addressed these words to his dad: "You may be wondering why today's program is all Beethoven. It's not because I thought a deaf composer was best suited for a partly deaf listener. There was a deadline for this concert, and in a race between pancreatic cancer and my ability to learn music, it wasn't clear who might win. It's a sad time for us as we face losing you; meanwhile, the terrible things that human beings do to each other intrude into our daily news. Beethoven's music feels especially beautiful at such a time. Not just because it is consoling, though it is consoling. Not just because it gives an outlet to our grief and joy, though it does. It's that his music embodies what is best about us. It portrays our search for what is beautiful and true. It shows us groping our way through uncertainty and knocking our heads against a wall over and over until a door is opened. It explores grief, but celebrates joy. And it is inspiring that a person as lonely and unhappy as Beethoven gave us such joyous music, music that is full of faith in life."

He played first the third movement of Sonata #29, the "Hammerklavier," followed immediately by parts of Sonata #21, the "Waldstein." Introducing them he spoke of the pain, frustration and anger expressed in these pieces and how these matched some of his own feelings. After a brief intermission, he then played Sonata #32, Beethoven's last, speaking of the gratitude he finds in the last movement and inviting the audience to hear in its themes the words, "Thank you, Lord . . ."

And Wayne, who had for weeks not been comfortable in one position for fifteen minutes, sat in that recliner for more than two hours, alert to everything, listening to the music and soaking up the love of guests as they arrived and then left. This seemed miraculous and was an answer to our prayers.

That was Monday; he lived until Friday, now and then weeping and declaring himself the most blessed man in the world.

I called my friend Hazel who lives two thousand miles away. I had not seen her for about twenty years. A long time ago, when we were about eighteen, I "stood up" with Hazel when she got married. There were five of us there, including the minister.

On the phone she said, "When are you coming?" I laughed. She told me that she had bladder cancer and was doing chemo.

I told her that travel is harder now that I am eighty-nine. She said, "Then you need to come soon, while you can, while I'm still here."

I confessed that my son was asking if I would like to go anywhere that he could take me. And it did occur to me that I might like to see my hometown one more time.

She said, "I will be ninety on April 17."

I said, "Well, I will be ninety on May 16."

She said, "Come in between, and we will have a birthday party."

We did it. I saw my hometown one more time.

245

The house where I was born was gone, a concrete slab in a vacant lot remaining. A man sauntered over from next door to see who we were and told us that the house burned several years ago. I stood in this vacant space and told stories, of sleeping in Zell's big featherbed in the loft, about John's tree with the peeling bark I was not supposed to pull off, and going to the ice house with Calvin in his little car.

The visiting neighbor wondered if I ever crossed the creek behind the house, and I told him I was not permitted anywhere near that creek. That reminded me though. A little house over there burned one night. I just remember that Zell's daughter, Louise, was holding me, wrapped in a blanket, and Mother was holding Betty Dean. We were all standing in the street, watching the flames that lit up the night. There was a fire truck spraying water on our house and Zell's. It was too late for the shack across the creek. Part of this memory, anytime it comes to me, is a feeling of security, warm in the blanket, hugged by Louise who kept saying in my ear that we were safe.

Two and half blocks away I found the house, an old and shabby house now, where once our family was quarantined while I was away at school. Betty Dean had diphtheria. I was sent to Zell's house, a place I loved to go. Zell boiled my clothes and ironed them. Morning and afternoon I walked past my own house, forbidden to come home.

In my second grade reader we had come to a story about Patsy and Paul going to an orange orchard. There were pictures of the orchard, unimaginable to this Arkansas child. In this pre-four-color-printing era, each orange was a perfect round ball, pure color against the solid green of the tree.

It was my habit to read to my little sister from my schoolbook, the only books we had. The next day I had to give this book back to the school, and Betty Dean had not seen it yet. But I had a plan. I stopped at my house, instead of just walking past. I told my daddy through the closed window that I would leave the book so they could show it to my sister and tomorrow morning I would pick it up again. But Daddy said that if he took the book he could not give it back. They would have to burn it to kill the germs so no one else would touch it and get diphtheria.

I tried all the way to Zell's house not to cry. The effort made my throat hurt. I told Zell who got scared and all evening kept holding my tongue down with a spoon handle and shining a flashlight into my throat.

I found five classmates still living there where we grew up, plus Hazel whose daughter and son-in-law brought her from Little Rock, and three other people, a bit younger, who remembered me and wanted to come to a gathering. We said to one another things like, "I would never have recognized you," and "You are looking great." We summarized long stories about our lives. We ate birthday cake.

That's a mountain peak on the landscape, visible from far away. By my going, by eating together and cutting cake, we claimed the survival of friendship; we planted a flag.

If old age is a time to look back and realize what was remarkable or life-changing or fun or sweet, whatever made us proud or happy, even perhaps what needs to be buried, then it is a time to look at the whole of it and celebrate.

I Will Bless My Grandchildren

We didn't want our eightieth birthday celebration to be all about the past. We wanted to celebrate what we have contributed to the future. So in the afternoon of that second day we blessed each of our ten grandchildren in a formal sort of ceremony.

We did it with a sense that they will live in a perilous time, equipped only with their natural gifts and what their parents and grandparents have given them. We wanted them to know at least that we believed in them and prayed for them while we could. And, of course, we had taken this idea from examples in Christian scripture.

Beginning with the eldest, we called each of them to stand in front of us as we read a summary of their personalities and gifts as we understood them. Then we asked them to kneel as Wayne read the special prayer written with that one person in mind.

Ten years have passed since this event, and all of us have grown, achieved, evolved. In the process these ten young people have made us proud, worried us sometimes, entertained us always and blessed us with their love. In addition they have brought into our lives a great many other people. While catching all ten of them in one room is nearly impossible, inviting them is scarily fun, because there is no way to predict how many other people they will bring. (This is a family habit; we are always moving over, adding plates to the table. We collect honorary members.)

Professionally they are an eclectic bunch: a mechanical engineer, a nurse, a soldier, a business consultant, an electrical company manager, an elementary school teacher, a motorcycle racer and an environmental specialist, while two are still students becoming a dietician and a vet. Who they are is so much more than what they do.

I am sure the world is better because they are in it, though I am often fearful and depressed about the troubled future they are walking into.

Recently I saw a cartoon by Steve Sack of the Minneapolis Star-Tribune. In this drawing a small boy is driving a child's car, pulling behind it a flat-bed trailer. On the trailer is a huge ball: Planet Earth on fire. On the front of the car there is a sign, "Ask me about my grandparents." On the boy's face is a determined scowl.

Mr. Sack has succeeded in expressing a deep fear of mine: that my generation has failed in numerous ways to address the issues of our time. We have set careless and selfish precedents. We have made excuses for problems that were ours to solve, and we owe our grandchildren apologies for passing to them situations made worse by our selfishness and laziness.

The least we can do now is to acknowledge our mistakes and beg for them God's wisdom and favor. Such actions carry our hope, our trust, our faith in their character.

Blessing our grandchildren, celebrating their existence and their potential, was the best part of our birthday, changing the focus from the past to the possible.

Ten years later we see the printed copies of these blessings hanging on the walls of their bedrooms. This is important. Though none of us can ever be sure where we are going, it helps to remember where we came from.

I Will Say Goodbye

Forty-eight years ago I had a friend who was dying. Not only was Virginia a friend, she was someone I looked up to, someone with character and intelligence and importance to the world. I have mentioned her already in another context. She was responsible in our mission for the work of Christian publishing in the Arabic language. Living a selfless life of service to others in Beirut, she was dying of cancer at the age of forty-two!

From our home in Amman, I had accepted writing assignments from Virginia and served on a committee that helped her make decisions about the small publishing program. I could not imagine this work continuing without her. For a long time I simply denied that it would happen. I thought we must not give her up. God would not let her die.

Evidence to the contrary piled up. Never before had I experienced so painfully the apparent random nonsense of death. It seemed an outrage. I questioned God, begged God, raged at God. If it was going to happen, I wanted there to be, at least, some logic, some explanation, and I got nothing.

Finally I wrote a letter to Virginia herself. I told her, "I need help. I don't know what to do with this."

And she answered. All she said, as I remember, was that we live in a fallen, sick world, and cancer is just part of it. No one is immune, she told me. But the words helped, because the acknowledgement that she was dying came from Virginia herself.

This and other experiences caused me some years ago to decide that people who are dying and know they are dying hold all the power, in a sense, and must help the living to deal with the situation.

I remember a conversation I had with Bill Bean, who was a Navy chaplain and the husband of my dear friend, Marie. "To die without admitting it to my family would be like boarding the battleship without saying goodbye. How could they bear it, if I left like that and never came back?"

It was only a few months later when I received a letter from Marie telling me that Bill had fallen suddenly and violently sick with pancreatitis and lived only three days. He had time to call Marie and their three teenagers to his hospital bedside, where he told them the truth, expressed his love and said goodbye.

It is wonderful to remember Bill Bean as a man who practiced the wisdom that he talked.

In the Middle East there is a common medical view that the terminally ill patient must be protected from the truth. If we admit that she is dying, we will take away the only thing on her side, her hope.

Because of this I have seen young people unable to say goodbye to their mother, though they knew she was dying. She herself knew but was not supposed to know, so she turned her face to the wall, rather than talk about it.

One day in our little town in California, when I saw my friend Carol at her place of business she was hurting because a woman she felt close to, one with whom she had shared many happy experiences, had been hopelessly ill for a month. And the first Carol knew of this was from the announcement that the woman had died. Not only had she told no one of her illness, but she had requested that there be no memorial.

Carol was deeply hurt that her friend had been unwilling to share with her the tragedy of her illness, unwilling to let her be warned of what was to come, and then unwilling to let her come to a service and express her grief or celebrate her friend's life.

I listened to this story, watched Carol wiping tears, and tried to express sympathy, but for a while did not know what to suggest that might help Carol get past this. Finally, I told her, "I think you should sit down tonight and write a letter to your friend; say all of the things that you would have said at her memorial, given a chance. And tell her some of your favorite memories of things you did together. Tell her thanks for all that, but tell her, too, how hurt you are now, and why. And say goodbye. You need a chance to say goodbye."

From perhaps extreme cases such as these, I have come to understand that dying is our final opportunity to give something to our loved ones, satisfying memories and peaceful hearts.

Because I have not been there, I can't know how hard that might be. If I am physically sick or in pain, will I find the strength to apologize, or grace to forgive?

Maybe not. This is why, if I need to do these things, I should not wait until the end is in sight.

But surely, in illness and pain, I can admit that it is time to say goodbye.

My husband and I knew for several months that he was dying, and we were surprised that knowing was such a blessing. The family knew; we were able to talk about it together. We gathered at Christmas, expecting that it would be the last Christmas that our family would be whole.

When it was time for Sam, one of our grandsons, to return to Virginia where he was in his last year of grad school, we gathered at the door so that Wayne could say a parting prayer for him. Then the rest of us stayed inside as the two of them walked out to the front yard and shared a goodbye hug. Watching from my kitchen window, I saw Sam walk to the door of his car, his face contorted in pain. He threw his jacket into the back seat, then turned and saw his grandpa still standing there near the step, watching him go. He came back, and they put their arms around one another again and wept.

I would not like to remember it any other way.

I am afraid to make promises I may not be able to keep, but it is my hope to make my dying, my sudden absence, as easy as possible for those who don't want me to go.

This is the last good thing I can do for my children and my friends. I will say goodbye.

I Will Trust God with The End

Since childhood, since the trauma of the strange white face in his casket and my refusal to believe this was John, a grandfather-sort-of-friend whom I adored, I have gradually learned it. Everybody dies. Everybody.

My grandparents died. My parents died. Two sisters. Aunts, uncles, cousins. Best friends. Neighbors. My life companion.

Devout Christians. Skeptics. Pagans. They all died.

Paupers. Rich people. No difference.

The elderly. Little kids. Newborns.

The prepared. The unprepared. The never guessing.

They were here and disappeared, leaving behind loved bodies that we were obliged to dispose of in some honorable way. I live, we all live, with the empty spaces they used to occupy, handle objects they valued, hear their words still in the air.

Some of them left big holes in our lives.

We think of them and wonder.

Some went expecting annihilation.

Others imagined an amorphous, dreamless, unconscious sleep from which they would never wake.

Others expected a grand homecoming and release from every hardship of life on earth.

And sometimes they are still here, big as life for a moment and then gone again. We even sometimes speak to them.

The departure of so many valuable people can only make us think.

How do I prepare for my turn to leave? How do I deal with the grief I feel about my own inevitable death? The instinct to live is powerful. In response to physical failures, we fight back. Until we can't anymore.

Under a death sentence, in suffering, my husband said, "Please, don't give me any more pills. Just let me go."

But then I watched him grieve; he would cry holding my hand and say, "These tears are for you. I don't want to leave you alone."

And suddenly he would remember the promises of the Christian faith and become happy.

One day he asked me to go to our basement library and bring up the oldest hymnbooks I could find. I brought six or seven, and he searched them all for songs he remembered from childhood. He chose ten that he wanted to be sung at his memorial. (I did not have the heart to tell him that there would not be time for ten, four-stanza hymns.)

Then at bedtime one night he said to me, "Tomorrow I want to sing to you the songs I have chosen."

And he did. He sat in his big recliner, so gray and thin already, but so alive still, and sang them in his aged tenor, many of them hymns I did not remember. One of them, "That Will Be Glory for Me," he could not get through all the way. Again and again he tried, but his voice would fail when he came to the words, "When by his grace I shall look on his face. . ." Every time he would weep at the unbearably amazing thought that he would see the face of Jesus, who promised his disciples, "I go to prepare a place for you . . ."

The promise was so real, the expectation so great, that he began to think of precious people who had preceded him and to get visibly excited. He named them: his parents, his brothers Ronald, Dwight, and Bruce, his sister Lois, dear friends. And one day he came to me in the kitchen to exclaim, "I'm going to see your mom and dad, and Scott and E.B. and Betty Dean and Joyce!" I was so touched that he anticipated seeing my family, too. Should I have sent messages?

The closer I am to being the one on the rim of departure the more I am sure that I am going to be surprised. Wonderfully, joyously astonished.

The literal truth, I am convinced, is that the reality that Jesus calls on us to believe is inexpressible in any language we know.

Even when talking about an earthly experience, the Bible uses metaphor after metaphor to describe the new life available to those who believe. The experience is like being on trial, knowing you are guilty, and then the judge sets you free, or like facing death and then someone takes your place. It is like being sold as a slave, then someone buys you and sets you free. And my favorite: being a fatherless, motherless child adopted into a big happy family. And so many others. Jesus speaks of a treasure found in a field, a light in the darkness, bread for the hungry, the lost being found.

This is why I feel that the truth is beyond all language. And what I expect is to be totally blown away by the unimagined.

Jesus did say specific things about how to be ready: "Don't be afraid." Over and over and in many situations, he said that. He said it when talking about the end. "Don't let your heart be troubled."

My life on earth has had enough frightful things: snakes and spiders, fire and loss, bombs and bullets, tornadoes, oncoming trucks, and unknown men walking behind me. As an imaginative and fearful child, I found something to hang onto in Psalm 56:3: "When I am afraid I will trust in you." This was the very first fragment of scripture that I internalized and appropriated. I memorized it. I whispered it lying in my bed in the suspicious dark. I said it later in young adulthood, sitting by the bed of a sick child. I said it in Beirut while hiding from falling shells.

I say it now. When I am afraid . . . I will trust. I trust that God is good. I do.

In consideration of possible options, I have decided over and over to believe Jesus and the psalmist who, long before the time of Jesus, praised God in a song (Psalm 13:5), saying, "I trust in your unfailing love."

For so many years the message of love has blessed and never failed me. Facing an appointment to travel, leaving behind everything else, this is what I have. I find it enough.

Today I Am Ninety!

Impressed with myself, I woke too early, read some messages on my phone and decided to go back to sleep. Well, actually I felt a bit anesthetized and drifted away again. That's why I didn't have breakfast until 10:00 A.M. But I had a little party in my heart while putting honey on my toast.

It rained in the night, and now the sun and the clouds are struggling for domination. The competition proceeds in streaks, like an NBA game. The morning is unseasonably cool, and because I left a window open all night, the cold inside is now equal to that outside. If I were a robust eighty, I would have just put on a sweater, but I thought that maybe now, in light of my advanced age and celebratory mood, I could pamper myself, so I turned on the furnace.

Actually I washed my white jeans yesterday, especially so I could wear them today with my new T-shirt, which is blue with white letters. The words identify me as a "Vintage Original 1929. Limited Quantities, Hand Crafted for Durability and Strength."

Even if it snows today that's what I'm wearing for my official ninetieth birthday snapshot.

Jeremy and John, two exceptionally loyal young men, are coming to visit in the afternoon, and I need to look my best. In the evening Nancy and Eileen are bringing Chinese, and we will eat in the dining room with a tablecloth.

This year my special day is like the conclusion of a long celebration that includes that long trip back to the town where I began, a feast on Mother's Day, gifts and cards in the mail all week, and a little surprise party at the end of Bible study yesterday. While writing these words, I received roses, red, white and yellow, delivered to my door. All this time everybody has acted confident that I would make it until this day.

"Making it" has been a trend in my life.

On our fiftieth wedding anniversary our son Jim stated that Wayne and I were still together mainly because we didn't get a divorce.

Using his principle, I admit I am still here because until now I didn't go somewhere else. I also have to acknowledge numerous opportunities.

For instance, in May 1947 the senior class of Wynne High School took a trip to a well-known campground. Harrell, a popular and handsome boy, brought with him, in direct disobedience of his father, a small pistol. When he came over from one of the boy cabins to our next door girl cabin, he knocked on the door and said something planned and trite like, "This is a stick up," to somebody who opened the door. We five girls reacted in various ways to this common expression. Anyway, the exciting part was not the gun but Harrell, because no boy was supposed to be in any girl cabin.

Amidst the general dither, Lucy said, "Harrell, let me see," and took the little gun. In my memory it lay in the palm of her hand. I lost interest and turned aside just about the time she pulled the trigger. The sound was definitely a surprise but small, like the gun. The bullet, without my immediate recognition, entered the pocket of my jeans from the side, passing through the edges of my slightly curved billfold twice, before burying itself in a wall. Later in the privacy of the toilet, I found that it had left a red streak on the skin of my groin.

It was Harrell who seemed in danger of dying, and, after she thought about it, Lucy, who had thought the gun a toy.

We five girls and the five or six other boys in the adjacent cabin (who somehow in the confusion showed up) all swore to keep this incident a secret, because we had never before seen Harrell the color of ashes, and because he was saying over and over, "My daddy is gonna kill me."

We kept our promise. Like nervous sentries, we guarded our words, knowing there was no one in that town we could trust with such a story. I, of course, had a problem no one else had: how to explain the holes in my jeans. At great expense to my conscience, I told my mother a carefully constructed lie. She looked confused, shrugged and never mentioned it again.

Fifteen years went by. I suppose it helped that we soon graduated and scattered to jobs, colleges, new ways of life. Finally, at a class reunion, Harrell, now grown up to be a solid citizen, stood up in the banquet hall, with my agreement, and announced that it was time to reveal all. And we told the story to our stunned classmates. The story itself was to them plausible; how they had never known was past believing. Lucy was happy now; she could finally cry in public from relief that she had not killed me. I confessed all to my mother.

Until now this secret maintained by no fewer than ten silly-kids-suddenly-turned-serious is legend; it came up at our celebration of survivors a few days ago, after seventy-two years. I repeated Harrell's words and someone said, "He would've. Mr. Brawner would have killed him."   I trust that they were speaking euphemistically.

What I feel sure of is that we all learned something about the fragility of life and the beauty of survival, things we would appreciate even more down the road. Just maybe some of us even noticed the superior wisdom of our elders.

It was not, of course, the last opportunity I had to be grateful for life.

In 1967 I had a fibro sarcoma in the muscle of my arm and felt fortunate not to lose the arm. The cancer never recurred.

In 1975 I crossed the volatile "Green Line" dividing Beirut to save a nearly finished manuscript and two copies of every title we had published. This venture was deemed necessary because of the possibility that our storehouse would be destroyed in the expected siege of West Beirut. On my way back across, one gunshot broke the silence. Maybe it was just a warning, but, besides the crack of the rifle, I heard the zing of the bullet when it ricocheted off something near me.

Uncounted times in the next few years we went up to our flat roof after artillery attacks and filled a shoe box with shards and chunks of shrapnel. Sometimes the concussion broke a window or two.

There was a massacre of Christians in a town whose roofs we could see from our windows.

In 1985 I had cancer of the colon and was very sick following surgery. Rumors of my imminent death were rational and circulated by some of my best friends, but proved to be untrue.

Still in my future was a head-on collision that, in the final second, didn't quite happen.

These are just examples of the opportunities I have had to leave earth early. Planet Earth is a dangerous place.

So many times I have pondered the mystery that I lived when others in the same circumstances did not. I have found nothing to brag about but every reason to be thankful. I mention this often to the Giver of every good and perfect gift, knowing that I am not loved more than others.

And though right now the sun is clearly losing its contest with the rain, I am going to wash my hair, and put on those white jeans, and celebrate that I am ninety years old.

Made in the USA
Monee, IL
01 February 2020